the essential guide to
PAINT &
COLOR

bay books

CONTENTS

the essential guide to
PAINT &
COLOR

Paint Products

The selection of paints, varnishes and other decorating products available can be confusing. These pages will help you to find your way through the maze of products and will guide you to the correct selection for the project you are undertaking and the surfaces on which you intend to apply it.

Paint is colored pigment suspended in a medium that makes it spreadable and gives it an acceptable drying time. Paint also contains the relevant chemicals to ensure that it does not rub off easily and that the color will not fade too much. It is often helpful to understand how paint is manufactured. There are two main processes involved: one for water-based paints and one for alkyd-based paints.

WATER-BASED PAINTS

Water-based paints are known as emulsion paints. They are water soluble and are made by pushing ground pigment (color in its purest form) into a solution of water and polyvinyl acetate (PVA) resin. PVA is a type of plastic. The pigment is forced into the resin and water at such high speed that it breaks up and disperses evenly. When you apply a PVA paint to your walls, you are effectively applying a skin of colored plastic and water. Once the water has evaporated, you are left with an even coating of colored plastic. The greater the shine on the PVA paint, the higher the ratio of plastic to water.

ALKYD-BASED PAINTS

Alkyd-based paints, such as satin and gloss, are more complicated to make and, as a result, are more expensive to buy. You can expect alkyd-based paints to last much longer than many water-based ones. Alkyd-based paint is made by first making a 'binder', which is a mixture of linseed oil, acid and alcohol. To this are added some thinners (white spirit) and ground white pigment, and this is then mixed. The pigment does not break up and disperse during this process so the mixture is then ground in a mill to ensure that an evenly whitened paint base results. Finally, some more thinners are added, along with a chemical drier and some stainers. The product goes through a staining process before it is officially called paint. You may be familiar with paint base; this is the product to which the DIY stores add stainers in order to color the paint to your requirements. So, when you apply alkyd-based paint you are simply covering your surface with colored oils. As it contains all these chemicals you can understand why it smells so powerfully.

PRIMER

Primer can be either water- or alkyd-based. It is used on bare wood to seal the surface and prevent the wood from swelling when the undercoat and top coat are applied.

UNDERCOAT

Undercoat can be either water- or alkyd-based. It is a thin surface preparation and is used to seal walls and woodwork before the top coat. It has a flat finish.

ACRYLIC LATEX FLAT PAINT

Acrylic latex flat paint is practical and inexpensive to use for covering large areas quickly. As it is water-based, it does not have an offensive smell and has no shine at all. Flat paints are difficult to wash if they become dirty but they can be touched up very quickly and easily. But there are now some washable acrylic latex paints on the market that help to overcome the difficulties of keeping a surface that is flat-painted looking like new.

ACRYLIC LATEX VELVET PAINT

Acrylic latex velvet paint is much the same as acrylic latex flat paint but easier to clean if it gets dirty and has a slight shine to it. For creating paint techniques your base coat must have a slight shine so this type of paint is recommended in place of flat finishes.

SATIN PAINT

Alkyd-based or satin paint has a good satin shine to it and usually also has a greater intensity and luster of color. It is more expensive than acrylic latex paint but will last at least twice as long. Satin paint has an offensive smell and it is recommended that, when using it, you work in a well-ventilated area to prevent inhalation of the fumes. Satin paint also takes longer to dry than water-based paints. However, the effect of alkyd-based paint on a surface is more professional than water-based paint.

GLOSS PAINT

Gloss paint is almost always alkyd-based and has a full gleam to it. It is quite difficult to apply and should be carefully brushed over a surface in two or three thin coats using a good quality brush. Over time, the shine of the gloss will reduce and the surface may need re-painting.

RADIATOR PAINT

Radiator paint has a lower quantity of ingredients that may yellow with heat. It also contains ingredients that prevent the paint peeling off a hot surface or softening when the radiators are on. Radiator paint is much more expensive to buy than other paints and the choice of colors is rather limited. However, if you are prepared to re-paint your radiators as time goes by, then you can use any shade of satin paint. Remember when painting always to work on a cold surface.

METALLIC PAINT

Metallic paints are made by suspending ground-up pieces of metal in a paint base and they give excellent coverage, though they must be stirred thoroughly and regularly. A line, like a watermark, may show between each brush or roller stroke but this can be rectified by working back over the area with a soft brush.

TILE PRIMERS

Tile primers are designed for those who cannot afford the luxury of new tiles when changing the room decor. You can safely and effectively paint over your old tiles for a new look. Apply tile primer in two coats, leaving at least 16 hours between each coat because it dries very slowly. When the primer is dry, you can paint the tiles in any color you choose, using an satin paint for a long life.

UNIVERSAL STAINERS

These take the form of a liquid colored stain that can be added to water-based or alkyd paints in order to adjust the color. It is available in traditional artists' colors. Try raw umber for 'dirtying' a color. Avoid black unless you are seeking a graying effect; it can be too artificial.

THEATER PAINT

Although theater paints are not intended to offer long-term coverage, they are now available in a range of diverse and intense colors, making them very appealing to more adventurous decorators, Used in the home environment, the paints should be stabilized with the addition of acrylic binder, which helps to ensure greater durability. Theater paints dry to a completely flat finish.

VARNISH

Varnish is just like paint but is clear. Most varnish goes through the same initial production stages as clear gloss does. Silicon powders are then added to make a satin or flat finish. These powders settle in the can so stir the varnish well before, and regularly during, use. Varnishes that claim to bring out the beauty of your wood may have some yellow colorants added to them. You can stain varnish easily for your own use by stirring in some artists' colors. Use oil colors for polyurethane varnishes and acrylics for water-based varnishes. Generally, the thinner the varnish, the easier it is to apply and the better the quality of your finished work will be. Before buying varnish, shake the cans and choose the ones in which the contents sound most like water. Very thick varnishes, such as yacht varnish, look good after only a couple of coats but the coats are very difficult and time consuming to apply. It is preferable to apply four or five coats of a thinner varnish to create a smooth finish.

WOODSTAIN

Woodstain is most often used for coloring untreated or bare wood. It can be either water- or spirit-based. Woodstain soaks deep into the grain of the wood but is transparent so that the original grain will still show through. Apply the wood-stain in generous quantities and wipe the surface with a soft cloth when dry. Wood-stain does not actually protect raw wood and you must apply a coat of varnish or wax over the surface after coloring it, for protection.

WAX

Wax offers an easy way to bring some protection and sheen to wood. Wax will nourish and protect most wooden surfaces and can be repaired and touched up easily. Beeswax is still one of the best wood polishes (and also smells very pleasant). All you need to do is apply the wax just like a floor polish, leave it to dry and then buff with a soft cloth. Re-apply wax on a surface from time to time as the sheen dulls. Waxes containing colorants are also available; these will stain the wood as you go. You may need to carry out several applications of colored wax before you achieve the color shown on the can. For the initial treatment of wood with wax you may benefit from hiring a professional buffer, such as those used to polish cars.

GLAZE

Glaze is another medium that can be colored for use in creating special paint effects such as ragging and dragging. In simple terms, it makes the color slippery and moveable. The glaze is applied with a paintbrush or roller and then, while it is still wet, it is manipulated (see pages 13 and 31–41) with brushes, rags, plastic or anything you like. When the effect is achieved, the glaze is left to dry and the paint effect will last for as long as ordinary paints. Glaze is available in alkyd- or water-based forms; the alkyd-based glaze has more luster and depth to it. When using glaze, take care to complete an entire section in one rapid session as, if the glaze begins to dry at the edges, you will see a significant 'watermark' where the over-laps are. Stop in corners only, having brought the glazed section to a neat finish.

ENAMEL AND CRAFT PAINTS

These paints are sold in small quantities and are useful for small jobs, detailing and murals. Their colors are very intense. Most enamels do not need to be protected with varnish and will keep their color for years. Craft paints, on the other hand, may be water-based and might resist a surface that has been prepared in oils. Always buy the best craft paint you can afford. The color in cheap craft paint can fade rapidly.

ARTISTS' OIL CRAYONS

These crayons are just like children's wax crayons except that they are oil-based. They can be used for touching-up jobs and for drawing fine lines where a paintbrush may be too bold, heavy or difficult to handle. An oil crayon can be sharpened to a point just like a pencil, and the color can also be thinned or smudged with the aid of white spirit.

PURE PIGMENT

Sold in powder form by art supply shops, pure pigment is the base of all the traditional colors on an artist's palette. The color of pure pigment is the most intense available and it can be mixed into either alkyd- or water-based products. It is expensive but you only need a small amount as you will not use that much at a time.

LINSEED OIL

Linseed oil can be used to make your own transparent paints by mixing with artists' alkyd paints or pure pigments, a dash of white spirit and, very importantly, a few drops of driers. Use refined or boiled linseed oil to minimize the yellowing effect. Linseed oil does not dry without chemical help from driers.

DRIERS

An essential part of the kit, chemical additives can be added to alkyd paints to speed up the drying time. Be careful not to add too much; one teaspoon is sufficient for 1 liter (35fl oz) of alkyd-based paint. Any more than this may affect the shine of the paint and make it appear powdery.

SPECIAL SURFACE PAINTS

The range of paint products designed to overcome specific painting requirements is constantly growing. A look along the shelves in any paint store will reveal paints designed for floors, melamine surfaces, tiles, steel and so on. All are tried and tested before appearing in our shops and can be relied upon to perform. Many of these paints require special cleaning up after use and it is worth reading the can before purchasing, and it is often essential to buy the appropriate thinners to go with them. Consider scrapping the paintbrush after use because it may be less expensive than cleaning it with special chemicals. Few of the really specialist paints are water-based. Take care to store them upright and away from heat sources and dispose of the containers safely when you have finished with them.

Troubleshooting

THE COLOR IS WRONG

If you are not happy with the color you have applied, you could re-paint the room. Alternatively, if the color you have applied is fairly pale, consider glazing over it using a simple paint technique such as colorwashing or ragging. Your base color will be toned down by doing this but will still glow through the transparent glaze. If the color looks too dark you could try sponging one or two lighter colors on top. Your base color will show through but the whole effect will become lighter and mottled. If you are using two or more colors for sponging, use the lightest color last.

THE PAINT IS WAXY

Careless preparation can often prevent alkyd-based paint from drying, or cause it to dry with a waxy feel. If you are painting onto a wooden surface you must prime the surface first. Primers provide not only a smooth surface on which to paint, but also a base on which the top color will cure (dry and set) fully. If you have overlooked priming the surface, wash the troubled paint away with plenty of white spirit and wire wool, and start on a primed surface. If the paint is drying very slowly with a waxy feel to it, then you have probably applied the coats too thickly. The surface of the paint is beginning to dry and cure and is sealing in the moisture underneath it. If you can, leave the paint for a week and see if it dries. If the paint does not dry, scrape it off, wash the wood with white spirit and wire wool and start again.

THE PRIMER IS NOT DRYING

This is a rare problem and is usually caused by the primer having been applied too thickly. Primer should be thin and soak into the new wood when applied, to provide a smooth and even surface on which to apply the top color. If the room in which you are working is damp you may also encounter problems with drying. Try heating the room with a dry heat and see if the primer dries. If it still does not dry, scrape off the offending primer and begin again.

NOT ENOUGH PAINT

If you notice the potential disaster of your paint running out in good time, you can stretch your paint by diluting it a little with the appropriate thinner. You can also make sure that you use every drop of the paint that you have soaked your rollers and brushes with, rather than washing it away into the sink. Sometimes you can buy a small tester pot of emulsion color to help with that last square meter. If you are working with a color that you mixed for yourself, and which cannot be repeated, then one wall or section of your room will have to be painted in a harmonizing shade or color.

SAGGING

This occurs when the paint has been applied too thickly or each coat has not been allowed to dry fully before the next was applied. To deal with sagging paint you must first allow it to dry fully and then rub the offending areas down with wet-and-dry sandpaper (use it wet for best results) until it is perfectly smooth. Then paint the rubbed-down parts again using the same number of coats as you have used on the whole area.

CISSING

This term is used to describe the appearance of paint that is resisting the surface onto which it is being applied. It usually occurs when water-based paint, such as emulsion, is being applied onto alkyd-based paint. For large areas you will be forced to buy new paint in alkyd-based form. For smaller areas, try washing the surface with detergent and a light scouring pad to remove any grease that may be sitting on the surface. If the paint still resists, you will have to resort to using alkyd-based paint.

CRACKING

Cracking is caused when paint or varnish is applied over a base layer of paint or varnish of different elasticity before it has been given long enough to cure (which can take up to a month). For example, two separate brands of varnish may react with each other and form cracks. To deal with cracking you must allow the surface to dry fully and then rub it down ready for re-painting. However, you could consider leaving the cracking visible. It is a very popular ageing technique and many people seek this particular decorative effect.

DRIPS

Drips or 'nibs' in the dried paint surface are usually pure oversights before leaving paint to dry. Rub the dried drip away with fine sandpaper and re-paint the area. On high-gloss finishes you may need to apply a final coat over the entire area to disguise the patch where you rubbed away a drip.

Product	Quality	Thinners and brush cleaning	Use for	Apply with
Primer	Preparation for bare wood. Prevents wood from swelling	Mineral spirits or water (check the can)	Bare wood	Brush or small roller
Undercoat	Flat finish, thin surface preparation and sealer	Water or mineral spirits (check the can)	Walls, woodwork	Brush
Acrylic latex flat	No shine, general-purpose coverage	Water	Walls, new plaster	Large brush or roller
Acrylic latex velvet	Satin sheen, general-purpose coverage	Water	Walls, murals, base for glaze work. Not for new plaster	Large brush or roller
Satin	Satin sheen, general-purpose coverage	White spirit or mineral spirits	Walls, woodwork and metal	Large brush or roller
Gloss	High shine, durable	Mineral spirits or water (check the can)	Woodwork, doors	Good-quality brush
Woodstain	Color without varnish for bare wood	Water or white spirit	Bare or unvarnished wood	Lint-free cloth or brush
Varnish - polyurethane	Alkyd-based wood and paintwork protection. Choice of shine	White spirit or mineral spirits	Wood and to protect paintwork	Good-quality brush
Varnish - acrylic	Fast-drying protection for wood and paintwork. Choice of sheen. Non-yellowing	Water	Wood and to protect paintwork	Brush or roller

Number of coats	Washable?	Area per liter (one coat) Square meters	Notes	Drying time pre re-coating	Drying time final coat	Undercoat
I	N/A	I2 meters	Thin to a watery consistency. Rub down with sandpaper when dry	2–4 hours	N/A	No
I	N/A	I2 meters	Stir well. Rub down with sandpaper when dry	Alkyd based 8 hours. Water based - 2 hours	N/A	N/A
2	No	I0 meters	Do not stir and avoid frost	I–2 hours	8 hours	No, but dilute first coat for raw wood
2	Yes, soapy water. Do not scrub	I0 meters	Dark colors require 3 or more coats	I–2 hours	8 hours	Acrylic latex flat
2	Yes, household cleaners. Avoid ammonia	I5 meters	Stir well before and during use	8 hours	24 hours	Primer or commercial undercoat
2	Yes, household cleaners. Avoid ammonia	I2 meters	Slow to apply – use good-quality, bristle brush. Alkyd-based is more hardwearing	4–8 hours	24 hours	Primer
I or 2	No	8 meters	Apply generously with brush or cloth. When dry, wipe off excess with dry cloth. Stainers do not protect wood; always wax or varnish when dry	I–3 hours	I–3 hours	No
Up to 8	Yes, soapy water	I0 meters	Use thinned and apply several coats for the greatest luster. May yellow as coats build up	4 hours	24 hours	No
Up to 8	Yes, but do not scrub	I0 meters	Difficult to apply as evenly as polyurethane varnishes. Not as durable but quick drying and crystal clear. Do not use on alkyd-based paints	I hour	8 hours	No

Product	Quality	Thinners and brush cleaning	Use for	Apply with
Wax	Protection and shine for wood	N/A	Bare or stained wood	Lint-free cloth
Alkyd-based glaze	Transparent	White spirit or mineral spirits	Mix with artists' oil colors to make colored glaze for various paint finishes	Brush or roller
Craft paint	Intense colors for detailing and small areas	Various	Small craft projects	Soft brush
Artists' oil crayons and pastels	Intense, pure colors in stick form	Oil or mineral spirits	Detailing and drawing on walls, furniture or paper	N/A
Pigment	Intense colors	Water	Make homemade paints for colorwashing	Brush or roller
Car spray paint	Low or high sheen, hard-wearing, wide color range	Cellulose thinners	Stencils and basic coverage	Spray from the can
Glass paint	Transparent or flat	Acetone	Painting glass of all kinds. Transparent detail work	Soft artists' brush
Blackboard paint	Flat black, very opaque	Methylated spirits	Interior flat finishes, chalk boards	Brush
PVA glue	General-purpose sealer	Water	Walls or woodwork to seal or stick	Brush

Number of coats	Washable?	Area per liter (one coat) Square meters	Notes	Drying time pre re-coating	Drying time final coat	Undercoat
3	Yes, with more wax or soapy water	8 square meters	Apply just like shoe polish, buff with a soft cloth between coats. Pure beeswax best for new wood; re-wax often	3 hours	N/A	Woodstain (optional)
1 or 2	No	Depends on consistency	Good workability for ½ hour. Cheap way to extend color	6 hours	N/A	Alkyd-based satin base
1 or 2	Yes, do not scrub	N/A	Better quality than poster paints. Widely available in small quantities	½ hour	N/A	N/A
N/A	No	N/A	Allow to dry for 3 weeks or more before varnishing	N/A	N/A	N/A
1	Yes	N/A	Can be mixed with alkyd- or water-based products	N/A	N/A	N/A
1 or 2	Yes	N/A	Extremely hardwearing; wear a mask when spraying	1 hour	10 hours	Spray undercoat
1	Yes, do not scrub; check label	N/A	Brushstrokes always show up; beautiful vivid color selection	1 hour	4 hours	No
1 or 2	Yes, water only	10 square meters	Fast drying, easy to repair and patch up	1 hour	4 hours	No
1	Yes, soapy water	12 square meters	Dilute 1:1 with water. Apply with brush	1–2 hours	N/A	No

Preparation

Preparation for all decoration is very important. Although it can be very time consuming, good preparation is worth every effort as it will improve the finished result no end.

REMOVING DUST

After sanding make sure you have a clean and dust-free environment. Dust down the doors with a dusting brush, making sure that no fine dust is left in the corners or moldings. Then wipe over surfaces with a tack cloth. This is a small sticky cloth that can be wiped over a surface to remove any remaining dust. Unfold and refold the tack cloth, as necessary, for cleaner, stickier sections. Tack cloths are available at decorating shops in individually sealed packets. When you are not using the cloth, keep it in a sealed packet or it will dry out and lose its stickiness.

MASKING EDGES

Use masking tape to protect the worktop and any appliances in the kitchen from paint. Stick tape along the adjoining edge, but don't stick tape to the adjoining wall as this could pull off the paint with it. To paint edges of a wall, push a brush very carefully into the edge.

PROTECTING THE FLOOR

Even if you intend to be extremely neat and tidy in your decorating, always cover the floor well with dust or plastic sheets. Plastic sheets provide more protection as paint cannot leak through them, although they can be slippery to walk on. Cover the worktops with plastic at the same time for protection against spills.

PREPARING WALLS

All the walls in this book have been painted in flat water-based paint. Holes and cracks can be filled, sanded down and painted straight over in water-based paint. If you have newly plastered walls, allow a drying-out period of about six months as small hairline cracks will appear through the paint as the plaster dries out. Bare plaster should be sealed first. For color-washed walls, a rollered surface is the best to work on. Remember that imperfections will show up more once a colorwash is applied as will areas that have not been covered sufficiently. A common miss are the edges and corners that are painted in with a brush. Make sure that these areas are covered well.

ADHESION

Kitchen units and doors get so much wear and tear that any paint finish must not only be well sealed for protection but most importantly the paint must stick well to the surface and not chip off. Paint adhesion must be considered at every stage of decorating. It is no use sealing a finish with a tough varnish if the original coat of paint has not stuck sufficiently to the base coat.

The projects in this book have used water-based acrylic paint together with artist's acrylic paints. These particular paints can never be applied to an alkyd-based finish as they will just not adhere. The surface must be porous and primer is an ideal porous surface to paint on. To apply primer to most surfaces, rub down the surface well with sandpaper to provide a key for the primer to adhere, then apply the water-based coat. Always check the instructions for each product you use; they vary considerably. Wood and hardboard are the easiest surfaces to paint. Formica and laminated doors are the hardest. Many paint manufacturers do not advise painting such surfaces but it can be done if you rub the surface down well with sandpaper to provide a key before applying primer. Use tile primer on non-porous surfaces.

VARNISHING

Water-based paint is usually used on ceilings and walls, while satin and gloss enamel, which are much harder and tougher paints, are usually used on doors and woodwork. As water-based paint is not necessarily made for wear and tear, it may be protected with acrylic clear varnish. Remember to use the correct varnish for the type of paint you use. For the water-based finishes in this book, a tough acrylic dead flat varnish was used. Acrylic varnish is also available in satin and gloss finishes, but the dead flat seemed most appropriate for the finishes in this book. Acrylic varnish does not yellow in the way alkyd-based varnish will but it does deepen the color, even in the dead flat form. At least two coats of varnish are required for a good finish.

CLEANING SURFACES

Paint will not stick to a greasy and dirty surface so all surfaces should be cleaned prior to being painted. Sugar soap is a very powerful surface cleanser designed especially for use in the decorating trade. It is tough and cuts through grease, grime and nicotine. Wear rubber gloves at all times when using sugar soap, and protect work surfaces and floors from any possible spillage.

To use sugar soap, first check your individual product instructions, and add warm water to the sugar soap accordingly. Apply this mixture with a brush or a cloth to the surface to be cleaned and then rinse with clean water.

FILLING HOLES AND CRACKS

There are many different spackling compounds available for different applications. Spackling compound can either be bought in powder form to be mixed with water, or as a ready-made paste. Fine surface spackling compound is ideal for intricate repairs, but an all-purpose spackling compound should be used for deeper cavities. The spackling compound will tend to sink into a hole so fill over and above the hole to enable this to be sanded down to a flat finish afterwards. If the hole is particularly deep, fill as much as you can first with small pieces or chips of wood, and then use spackling compound for the remaining space. Instant flexible spackling compound is best for sealing sides and edges and areas prone to movement. It is applied through a tube and wiped smooth with a damp cloth. It cannot be sanded down and should not be used for surface holes. To apply spackling compound, smear a small amount into the hole using a filling knife. Leave to dry.

SANDING

Sandpaper is available in many different grades, from very coarse to very fine. If the paper you have is too coarse, tear it in two and rub it together to grind it down for a smoother abrasion. If you are sanding a whole door, start with a coarser paper (if required) and work up to a finer grade to finish.

Wet-and-dry sandpaper is good for achieving a super fine glass-like finish on a surface. This is only really applicable for alkyd-based semi gloss finishes and especially gloss paint. This very fine paper is used wet and rubbed onto the surface. You can wrap the sandpaper around a sanding block to make rubbing down easier. The sanding block in the photograph was bought from a decorating shop, and is made from cork, but you could use any very flat material such as a smooth piece of wood.

Once the spackling compound is completely dry, rub the surface down with sandpaper wrapped around a sanding block for a smooth and flawless finish. Wipe away any dust with a tack cloth.

Tools

ROLLERS

Use long-pile rollers for textured finishes or uneven surfaces, and short-pile rollers for a smooth finish. A foam roller is useful for a smooth finish with alkyd-based paints but may bubble or 'orange peel'; work slowly with a well-loaded roller to avoid this. The small rollers sold for gloss paint are a useful addition to any painter's kit as they can be cleaned more easily than larger rollers.

SANDPAPER

Available in different grades, sandpaper is used for rubbing down and also smoothing surfaces prior to painting, and for cleaning any drips of paint from a carpet.

ICE CUBE TRAY

Useful as a palette which holds a little sample of many colors at one time; it is easy to hold in one hand at the top of a ladder when painting detailing and murals.

PAINT PADS

These are wonderful speed painters, faster than a brush and smoother than a pile roller. Made from foam with a mohair painting surface, they are available in a wide range of sizes. Paint pads are more economical with paint and much easier to wash than rollers. Work in every direction adjusting the pressure from light to heavy as the pad runs out of paint.

TACK RAGS

These are sold as disposable cloths on a roll, or separately packed. They are lightly impregnated with spirits and oils and are perfect for wiping away dust after sanding a wooden item, prior to priming, painting and varnishing it. The oils and spirits can also help with cleaning paintwork prior to painting but sugar soap should be used if you are going to use a water-based paint.

TOOLS FOR GLAZE WORK

Not all glaze finishes are carried out with the aid of an expensive speciality brush. Plastic bags can be screwed up and used to create a leathery effect, corks can be jabbed in to the glaze for a fossil effect and rags used to create a soft mottled look. Experiment with anything that will not leave lint or fluff in the glaze—try clingfilm or foil and even the side of your fist or your fingertips.

PAINT TRAYS

These are not just for rolling paint, they are also useful for standing open cans of paint in and for mixing small quantities of paint.

DISPOSABLE PAPER PALETTE

Use this for tiny quantities of several colors at one time. The tear-off sheets eliminate any cleaning at the end of the day. Very comfortable to hold for long periods.

PAINT KETTLES

Sturdy and reliable containers for a tin of paint or a glaze mixture. A kettle can be hung from the top of a ladder with a meat hook or the handle. Keep an empty kettle handy for putting wet brushes in. Plastic kettles need not be washed after use and can be re-used after the paint has dried until eventually you throw them away. Steel kettles are more expensive and therefore require more care and cleaning.

MAHL STICK

This is a cane with a soft ball of chamois leather or cloth tied to the end. For high work that requires a very steady hand, hold the mahl stick in your non-painting hand, supporting the cane under your arm. Rest the ball on the wall. You can then rest your painting wrist on the stick and remain steady, even for minute details. You can make a mahl stick by attaching a cut tennis ball to one end of a can with a large square of chamois leather wrapped over the ball and tied securely to the cane.

Brushes

STIPPLING BRUSH

Use a stippling brush for removing brushstrokes and for creating a dotty stippled paint effect. Most decorators use stippling brushes about 5cm (2in) square. Larger stipplers are faster to work with but become heavy as the hours pass. Stippling brushes are expensive and can be replaced with a large emulsion brush from which the loose bristles have been carefully picked out. If you use an emulsion brush be sure to move it around as you work, in order to prevent the imprint of the straight edges from showing.

BADGER SOFTENER

A necessary expense for any serious decorative artist, this brush is made from very soft, long bristles of pure badger hair. Use it to tickle away brushstrokes from wet glazes and to give an out-of-focus appearance. It is essential for marbling work and useful in creating a colorwashed effect. Meticulous cleaning and conditioning is important as badger brushes are expensive to replace.

DUSTING BRUSH

This has endless uses, from dusting items before painting, to colorwashing and dragging. Natural bristle dusting brushes are more flexible and durable than cheaper, synthetic types.

WALLPAPER PASTING BRUSH

Use this large brush for smoothing wallpaper into position on a wall. It is wide and comfortable to handle for long periods at a time.

FLOGGER

This brush has extremely long, floppy bristles which, when gently tapped into wet glaze, create the distinctive flecks seen in natural woodgrains such as oak.

RADIATOR BRUSH

This is a standard household brush attached to a long-angled handle; it is helpful for painting behind radiators and pipework.

VARNISHING BRUSH

Not essential but a joy to work with, a varnishing brush looks just like a normal household brush except that it is only about 5mm (¼in) thick. The bristles are very flexible, hold a lot of varnish or paint and help to feather alkyd-based paints. This means that you can achieve a perfectly smooth paint surface with the minimum of effort.

ARTISTS' FITCHES

Usually made from hog's hair and quite stiff, fitches make excellent detailing brushes and are suitable for mixing small quantities of paint. The bristles of good-quality fitches are lightly curved in towards the top of the brush, rather than being unnaturally straight. However cheap versions can be used for most work – apart from murals.

FINE ARTISTS' BRUSHES

For detailing and fine mural work, a selection of medium-quality fine artists' brushes is important. Imitation sable or nylon work well and are less expensive than real sable or pony hair brushes. Store them in a tube or brush wrap; do not store soft brushes in a pot with the bristles pointing downward as they will bend.

DRAGGING BRUSH

This is a specialist brush with extra long flexible bristles for creating a fine striped effect. If you have a choice of dragging brush, always go for one with a comfortable handle.

HOUSEHOLD BRUSHES

A good selection of general household brushes is the starting point for any decorator. Buy the most expensive you can afford; cheap brushes will shed many hairs and not last long. Look out for a hole in the middle of the bristles which has been filled with a wooden wedge. This will fill with paint and the brush will drip.

SASH BRUSHES

Originally designed to help with the painting of complicated sash windows, sash brushes are available with pointed or rounded tips. They are perfect for edging and lining, and also for stippling paint on small areas or when control is required. With a little practice you will be able to apply paint in a perfectly straight line by using a sash brush. It may well become an essential part of your decorating kit and reduce your masking tape expenses.

LIVING ROOM
MAKEOVERS

Take a look at the colors you can see around you. Now, for a few moments, imagine a world without color. It's not easy. We use color automatically in our lives for pleasure, business and guidance. Road signs use color to offer us information or warn us of danger. Traffic lights tell us to stop or continue by using red, green and amber. Imagine the difficulties a world without color would pose to corporations bent on building at-a-glance identities, or safety organizations which rely on instant recognition.

The extreme of this use of color has to be advertising placards which no longer even mention the brand or product being sold to us. Yet the message is still clearly understood because of color association.

You will instinctively choose certain colors when buying clothes. Why? You will know that a particular color suits you, or maybe you are more comfortable in another. Perhaps the yellow of your shirt makes you stand out from the crowd. Color in the home can have exactly the same associations as the clothing you wear; it can relax or revitalize, warm you up or cool you down. It can even be anonymous, making way for your accessories and furnishings. The incredible transformation qualities of color are infinite and the choice is yours.

Although today's demand for color has led to a huge growth in paint colors available, it can be daunting knowing how to achieve the desired effect in the home or where to start when combining colors. Professional interior designers use their

knowledge and experience to make color and decorating choices that will work on a practical level as well as aesthetically. It is this type of advice and information that is included here. By concentrating on a single room, each title in the Makeover Series takes into account the very different color and paint considerations each room demands. This is very much in tune with the way interior decoration is approached, concentrating on the overall color choices for one room at a time.

This section should be used as a practical guide to selecting paints and colors for your living room, creating the desired environment. Discussion on color theory will enable you to follow the same processes as the professionals when choosing and using color in the home. Practical advice on paint products and their suitability is combined with inspirational examples showing the use of color in a room. This knowledge will allow you to manipulate your own space.

A room can look radically different when the

colors and paint finishes are changed. This is illustrated here by the different makeovers of an identical room. The same room was painted and accessorized six times. In these makeovers color is used in many different ways—as paint and on furnishings and accessories—creating an all-over look. The individual projects allow as little or as much of that look to be re-created or adapted to suit other decorative schemes.

Each makeover includes basic information on initial preparation and techniques, as well as advice on how to complete the different projects. By 'basic', we mean 'from the beginning' thereby allowing an absolute beginner in the field of home decoration to get to grips with putting ideas into practice. Everything you need to know to get started is contained within these projects.

All of the projects featured were completed within two days. If you allow four days, you will be able to work at a relaxed pace and enjoy yourself as well.

Using color in your living room

Paint and color in the home are only surface decorations, but they play an important role. Just as clothes, cosmetics and perfumes offer a snapshot of a personality to the onlooker, so the decorating schemes in homes and the atmosphere produced offer much the same. For example, the living room is usually more inviting than the study in the same house. It will, after all, be responsible for creating an atmosphere for the entire house.

COLOR AND MOOD

Color is believed to have an important psychological impact on mood, well-being, energy and motivation. Autumnal colors are considered to be relaxing and thus not suitable for offices, whereas peppermint greens are supposed to encourage alertness. It follows therefore that restaurants and bars favor warm autumnal shades, to relax the clientele and make them stay longer, while the gym at a leisure center is sure to be painted in a fresh pale tone to keep people awake, training hard, and going back time and again! In the 1980s, some corporate environments even employed bright garish colors in the cloakrooms in the hope that the colors would be daunting and discourage long conversations between members of staff behind the scenes, and in this way minimize time spent away from the actual workplace not making money.

Pattern, too, is used in some commercial environments to control actions. One of the major clothing chains in the United Kingdom laid carpets

The wall color in a room will always be the major influence on the overall atmosphere. The cool blue room (top left) has gone all the way with blue walls, woodwork and accessories, adding just a splash of brightening yellow in the curtains. The yellow room (bottom left) makes use of a jamboree of New England muted tones for the woodwork and accessories and yet still sings warm yellow.

19

with a herringbone zigzag pattern, running from the main doors into the store, in all of their large shops. This use of a subconscious guiding line encouraged customers to walk further into the store and thus see more of the merchandise on sale. It is quite probable that a lot more money was spent in the shops as a direct result of this manipulation by color and pattern.

MIXING COLORS

In today's world of color, the rules are continually being broken and experimentation is the key. In past years one would have heard a sharp intake of breath if colors such as orange and pink were used together. Now it may be considered daring, but that is all. It is certainly not against the rules; colors in your living room can be mixed and matched at will.

A color wheel offers a quick and easy way of combining colors for more timid designers. In fact, we are all familiar with the basic combinations and probably use them instinctively as colors which 'go' together. Black and white, for example, are opposites and an obvious choice where contrast is essential, such as on the printed page. If you take black and white down a little you will find navy blue and cream: colors which are quite simply stunning for home decor. A little further down will take you to tones of beige or yellow against reddish purples such as burgundy, which can be softer on the eye. If you are uncertain, the color wheel holds its own as a great adviser.

CHOOSING COLORS

The colors selected will be the primary factor in creating a mood or atmosphere. The living room is a tricky room to paint because, in most homes, it is a room which is used both during the day and in the evening. It may also serve different purposes at different times of the day. Maybe children play here, and perhaps it is used as a workspace during the day and a place to eat and relax in during the evening. In these dual-purpose living rooms the choice of color can be vital.

The blue room on page 68 was painted in order that it could be used for children during the day and still be a comfortable evening environment for adults. Although perhaps not as charming as the evening warmth of the creams used in the room on page 60, it is nevertheless clean and functional for all times of the day. It would be difficult to imagine children playing in a magnolia-colored environment when they would be better stimulated by bright primary colors such as red and green. Likewise, it would be hard

to relax in a primary-painted living room. The crisp pale blues used in this room are something of a compromise between the two requirements.

There are several factors to bear in mind when decorating and accessorizing your living room. First, consider how often the room is used and at what times of the day. If the living room is only ever used in the evening any color from the entire spectrum can be used. You may safely choose warm colors, such as terracottas and deep golds, and at the other end of the spectrum you may also select crisp clean whites and other accent colors. Second, you will need to consider lighting, and, third, the purpose and size of the living room before you launch into decorating.

Take some time selecting the colors for your living room. Perhaps even paint some large boards in what you believe to be your chosen color. Prop these boards against the wall and live with them for a few days in a variety of light conditions before making a final decision.

EFFECT OF LIGHTING

Natural lighting can limit your color choice. If your living room receives very little natural light, care must be taken not to make the room look too somber. Autumnal colors such as deep burnt oranges and terracottas can have this effect. Blues in a shady room can look cold, and white can look too stark and clinical. If, however, your room receives a lot of light and sunshine then you may like to capitalize on this fact and create a sunny haven.

Normal off-the-shelf light bulbs have a yellowing effect. If you take a good look at a white room in the evening, you will really be looking at yellows rather than whites. It is not time to change your lighting, rather consider it when choosing your colors. Most colors become warmer as yellow is added to them with evening lighting but beware of blues and purples which will become greener or grayer respectively, while reds become more orange. For a continued natural sunlight effect you could try the daylight simulation bulbs available from most stores, made from pale blue glass. Try only one to start with as you might find you prefer conventional evening lighting after all.

FUNCTIONAL CONSIDERATIONS

Before decorating your living room, consider its function. Does it serve as a dining room as well? If so, you might want to reflect this dual function in the color scheme. Perhaps your living room serves also as a play room or nursery. If so, you will be aware that color is not quite as important as washability and ease

of maintenance. It is possible to combine the two, however, if you select your paints carefully and go for quick-drying ones that you can touch up when required.

Keep a note of the exact name of the paint color you eventually select for your living room in order to be able to buy it again if you ever need to patch up areas of damage. Matching through guesswork is very difficult.

Also bear in mind that some paints are mildly toxic and should not be used in areas where children play.

If you are tinting your paints with tubes of artist's color, check the health label on each tube, as toxicity could be an issue. Watch out for the words 'cadmium' and 'chromium' on the color names.

The more hardwearing paints, such as satin enamel and gloss finish paints, will undoubtedly smell for a few days after application as the oils and thinners dry out. These more chemical-based paints will last longer, however, and have greater luster, so it could be worth the aroma as the price for perfection. Keep a newly painted room well ventilated and, most importantly, dry for a while; this not only helps to eliminate chemical smells but it will aid the drying and curing process and promise years of good service from your efforts.

ROOM SIZE AND COLOR

The size of the living room will also affect choice of color. Some colors 'recede' which means that they add to a feeling of space, while some 'advance' which can make a room look either smaller or more cosy, depending on how you use them. Red and green are

APPLE
Green

Good enough to eat and as vibrant a color as any in the spectrum, apple green often inhibits decorators with its sheer intensity. However, it is a good color in both daylight and evening light and works well with simple colors such as off-whites and purest white. Green also makes you feel hungry.

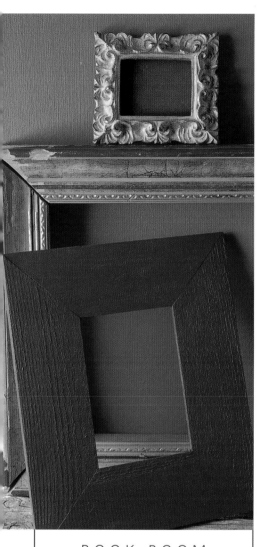

BOOK ROOM
Red

This deep red creates a feeling of warmth and relaxation and works well with gold. This color is not for tiny rooms as red advances but it is perfect for library-type living rooms, as its name suggests. A relaxing color with less kick than crimson or scarlet, book room red often appeals to men.

the most forceful examples of this; red advances and can make a room look smaller, while green recedes and can produce the opposite effect. Red against a green background advances so much that the effect is almost three-dimensional.

All the main makeover pictures in this section are of the same room. Although it looks completely different with the varying colors and tones, the dimensions of the room are the same. The cream room (see page 60) looks airy and spacious, while the brown room (see page 52) seems small and cosy. For an illustration of the most dramatic and surprising difference, put a finger in the section on the yellow room (see page 34) and on the pastel room (see page 26), and flick from one to the other a few times. You will see how the pastel room looks somehow longer and lower and the yellow room seems higher and wider.

The photographs were all taken at roughly the same time of day so lighting conditions cannot be used as an excuse. Neither were the paints shaded or changed on the walls of the rooms, which means that exactly the same treatment was used across an entire wall. In the brown room (see page 52) the shadows beside the window (on the back wall) were rather cool and gray compared to the warmth of the rest of the room. If this area of shadow had affected the entire wall, a lighter tone would have been used on the back wall to compensate for the coolness. Just one or two shades lighter on a paint chart will make a difference without being too noticeable.

A flat mirror above the fireplace reflects terracottas from the opposite wall with an added brightness and creates the illusion of an alcove and more space.

The pastel room (see page 26) looks long and narrow because the divisions between the various colors tell your brain to move along the walls or around the room. Thus your sense is of the width of the walls. In the yellow room (see page 34), with fewer divisions and a paint effect in the form of vertical stripes, your eyes are drawn up and down. A white ceiling is like a blank expanse of nothing to the brain so you look right up the yellow walls and onward into nothing, thus the sense of height is stimulated. Do bear in mind, however, that a white ceiling is not always the perfect finishing touch for a room as it can look unfinished.

DIVIDING COLOR

The way in which you divide color will also alter the effect in a living room. Many horizontal breaks, such as different colors above and below a dado rail, or above and below a picture rail, will serve to draw the eye along the walls and thus give a feeling of a lower ceiling. On the other hand, painted stripes running vertically draw the eye up and create a feeling of height.

The color of the ceiling is important. The paler it is, the higher it will look. If you are aiming for a warm feel, consider a cream or pale tone of one of the colors featured elsewhere in the room. For example, a pinkish-beige ceiling in a terracotta room will go almost unnoticed whereas a white ceiling will provide a stark contrast and draw the eye upwards. However, do take care with intensely colored ceilings as they can look rather amateurish: sunflower yellow on top of sky blue and pale yellow would not look very good.

SUNFLOWER
Yellow

Yellow is a color associated with cheerfulness. Deep yellows can be difficult to accessorize but work well with dark wood. Regal purple is the opposite color to this bright yellow; if these colors are used together they create a very rich atmosphere. Alternatively, use yellow with green for a garden feel. Look in a florist's window for inspirational ideas on how to mix yellow with other colors.

NEUTRAL
Naturals

Natural shades evoke a feeling of comfort in some people. The shades used in this photograph reduce the temperature and have a subtle outdoor feel to them. Rooms can be accessorized with other natural shades, such as baskets and dried grasses, or, alternatively, they work well with modern chrome. Naturals are as far as you can go towards autumnal shades without creating a cosy, warm air in a room.

COMPROMISING

There may be a dilemma to overcome between what you want the room to look like and what will serve the room best. For example, you might want a bright white room with a polished wooden floor. But this would not be practical for a cosy living room where you watch television and entertain friends, and certainly not if you have children. The color choice needs to be practical rather than dictated by emotions; compromise is essential, as is your choice of paint type. Sometimes the cost of a shiny finish will be prohibitive compared to the cost of flat paints. There may also be times when the washability of the paint is essential and thus a shinier surface is worth the extra cost.

Intense colors, such as deep greens and terracottas, will always look superb in evening light but consider how much they will be viewed in natural light. The effect can be completely different. It is advisable to try a test area first. Paint a large area going around a corner so that you can view it without seeing any of the original walls. Then look at it for several days in all light conditions before making a decision. Small patches of color will help you to know if you like the color but will not show you how the color will look in your room.

Colors can look different from the color card because of lighting and the effect of accessories and furniture. Shades of yellow in particular often cause a problem as they can look greenish.

Using a palette of mixed pastels creates an atmosphere of calm and serenity as long as the colors used are all of the same tone.

The Pastel Tones

This living room, which has been painted like a harlequin's jacket in four different colors, will challenge your ideas about color harmony, opposite colors and shade. The secret here is tone; all the colors used in this room are the same intensity as each other. The only rebel in the tonality is the deeper shade of purple featured in the rebated shelves.

The inspiration for the decorating scheme for this room came from various sources. The mixed

PROJECTS FROM
THIS MAKEOVER
SHOW YOU:

• *How to prepare an alkyd-based surface*

• *How to choose and use opposite colors*

• *How to paint a room without masking off*

• *How to make a box frame*

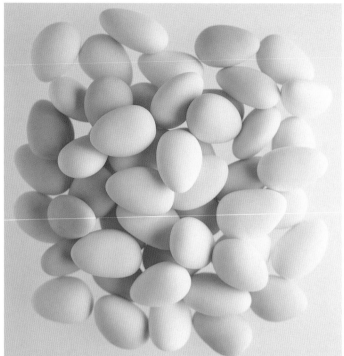

pastel colors are reminiscent of old-fashioned sugared almonds while the powdery finish is rather like pastel chalks. Look at the colors on a paint chart for ideas of colors to use.

Using pastel tones makes a room feel more spacious. The mixed colors work together to create an atmosphere of calm and serenity; using yellow for the ceiling against the blue of the side walls makes the ceiling feel lower.

The paint used has a flat finish, producing a somewhat powdery effect. To achieve the finish and to create the depth of color required will take several coats. Paint the walls first, then the skirting boards; there is no need to mask these as you can cover up rough edges later.

PREPARING AN ALKYD-BASED SURFACE

If your walls have previously been painted with alkyd-based paints, you will need to prepare them prior to painting with water-based emulsion. To do this wash down the surface with sugar soap or a solution of detergent and water, using a scouring pad. This will provide a 'key' for the water-based paint to grip. Even after this treatment, your first coat of paint may resist a little but the second coat will fill any gaps. You will need at least three coats of emulsion to cover an alkyd-based surface. Allow each coat of paint to dry thoroughly before applying the next one.

FINDING COMPLEMENTARY AND OPPOSITE COLORS

If you cannot decide on the combination of colors to use in your room, you need first to work out which colors go well together without clashing. Using the color wheel is a simple way of discovering complementary and contrasting colors. To find an opposite color quickly and easily, simply stare hard at the first color for a minute or so and then transfer your gaze to a white surface. Wait about 15 seconds and the opposite color will reveal itself—it's just like looking at a yellow sun and then seeing a purple dot in your vision, only safer.

THE COLOR WHEEL

The color wheel illustrates the basics of color theory. Colors directly opposite are negatives of each other and therefore work well to create contrast. Colors found in the same quarter are known as 'analogous' and harmonize as color families. Colors exactly one third apart on the wheel are called triadic and are a safe way of choosing a rainbow of colors without any clashing.

With red, for example, you can use green for contrast and more dramatic effect or orange and orange/red for relaxing harmony. The rainbow effect could be created safely by using red, yellow and violet.

Painting a room

This method of painting a room in different pastel shades ensures a quick transformation without the necessity of masking off each section as you work. After you have had some practice using this cutting-in technique on the first wall, the rest will be easy. You will be able to paint a room like this one wall at a time, leaving several days in between each wall without the end result looking messy.

1 Beginning at the corner of a room, use a small paintbrush to paint the edge of one wall pale blue. Don't worry about paint going over the corner on to the second wall. This will be painted over later in a different color.

2 Apply purple paint to the edge of the adjoining wall with a small paintbrush or varnishing brush. To achieve a neat edge, push the tips of the bristles into the right angle of the two walls, as shown. This is very easy and takes only a little practice.

3 Finish painting both walls using a paint roller and plenty of paint. Coat the paint roller in paint, then roll it over the wall to cover the surface. You will need three coats on each wall, allowing the paint to dry for one or two hours between each coat.

4 To paint clean sharp edges on rebated areas, such as the shelves in this room, apply the paint with a brush to within a few centimeters of the edge. Then paint up to the edges by pulling a loaded brush gently out of the rebate. Work slowly to avoid flicking paint every-where.

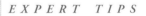

EXPERT TIPS

- *If your paint roller is not producing a smooth finish, this usually means that the pile on your roller is too long. Switch to a shorter pile or use a paint-brush, or apply the paint more thickly so that it 'settles' before it begins to dry. Watch out for runs when applying paint thickly.*

- *Do not apply alkyd-based paints thickly as they may not dry properly, resulting in a waxy skin on top and soft paint underneath.*

MATERIALS

- box
- sandpaper
- white primer
- household brush
- water-based paint
- display item for frame
- contact adhesive
- thin glass
- right-angled beading
  wood
- miter block
- saw
- wood glue
- masking tape
- picture wire and
  hanging
  fittings

Making a box frame

Hanging in the shelves at the front of this room is a little box frame which is a simplified version of the framing technique very popular in homes at the moment. This frame was quickly and easily made from an old sturdy box. Cigar boxes are ideal for this purpose. Some come branded with the cigar make and are attractive left unpainted.

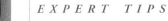

> **EXPERT TIPS**
>
> - *Sometimes these boxes come with sliding lids, in which case you could simply replace the lid with a piece of glass cut to size. If you prefer, you can use perspex instead of glass; it is lighter, but is more likely to scratch.*
>
> - *Mirror tiles placed in the bottom of the box can also work well if the back of the display item is attractive.*

1 Discard the lid and sand the surface of the box to a smooth finish. Paint the frame with a coat of primer, then, when dry, add a coat of water-based paint, reserving some of the paint for finishing, and leave to dry.

2 Insert the item to be displayed in the box frame. Secure it in place with a few drops of contact adhesive. Allow the glue to dry.

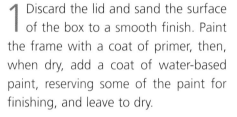

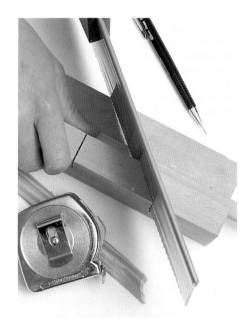

3 Have a piece of thin glass cut to fit the top of the box, so that it can be placed on the box without falling in. Saw lengths of beading wood to fit around the top edges of the box frame. Use a miter block to make neat mitered corners. Paint the beading to match the box frame.

4 Lay the glass on the box frame. To secure it in place, glue the beading onto the frame using wood glue. Hold the beading in position with masking tape while the glue dries. Fix picture wire to the back of the box frame with hanging fittings to complete.

Yellow is a popular color in decorating schemes, brightening and warming a room, and is a perfect backdrop to other colors.

Versatile Yellow

Of all the colors in the spectrum, yellow is one of the most popular and widely used in homes. It brightens and warms, does not change the feeling of space and can be used as a backdrop to so many other tones and colors.

Yellow looks wonderful both in natural light and in artificial light; yet it also looks different in both. During daylight hours a yellow-painted room looks fresh and clear while in the evening light it takes on warm 'oaty' tones, making it ideal for relaxing in. There are many shades of yellow you

PROJECTS FROM
THIS MAKEOVER
SHOW YOU

- *How to paint a smooth surface*
- *How to get straight lines*
- *How to drag a wall*
- *How to create other paint effects*

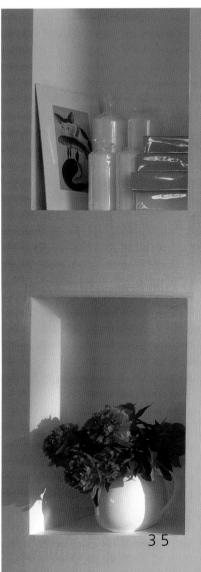

35

can base your decorating scheme on: the soft pale yellow of sponges, the sharp yellow of lemons, or the orangey yellow of sunsets.

This room is painted from floor to picture rail with a simple glaze technique called dragging. This effect is more formal and tidy than most other paint effects. Close inspection will reveal a thin stripe in the paintwork, no wider than a pinstripe, which subtly enhances the feeling of height in a room. A paler ceiling continues the effect and can really 'raise the roof'!

The background for dragging must be smooth and painted with a brush, not a roller. Keep the glaze as thick as cream.

PAINTING A SMOOTH SURFACE

The base coat for dragging must have a slight sheen to enable the glaze to slide around on top. Use either alkyd-based satin or water-based low sheen finish paints. To achieve a smooth finish, apply the paint generously with a brush in a criss-cross pattern on an area about a meter square at a time. Then gently feather the tip of your brush over the surface, finishing off with all brushstrokes in the same direction. Continue with the next square meter before the edges of the first have dried. This process is known as 'laying off'.

DRAWING GUIDELINES

It is difficult to create vertical lines around a room without eventually veering to the right or left with your brushwork. Once this has begun to happen it is very difficult to remedy and may continue to get worse as you work. You may not even realize it is happening until you reach a corner or stand back to look at your work. It is therefore advisable to mark the walls lightly with guidelines at intervals of 1 m (40 in) around the wall and then to follow these when dragging.

1 To draw vertical guidelines, hang a plumbline from the ceiling next to a wall (any weight suspended on a long piece of string can serve as a plumbline) using a pin or sticky pad. Lightly mark the true vertical on the wall with a ruler and a crayon in the color of your paint by running the crayon down the string. Repeat this at 1 m (40 in) intervals around the whole room before you begin to paint.

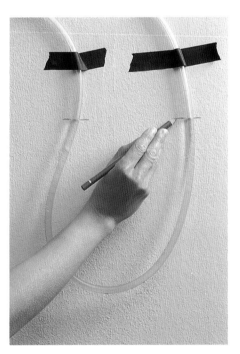

2 To draw horizontal guidelines, half-fill a 1 m (40 in) length of plastic tubing with water. Tape the two ends of the tubing to the wall so that the tube forms a 'U' shape. Using a crayon, mark the water level at both ends of the tube; they should be at equal heights. Then draw a line between the two marks. Repeat at 1 m (40 in) intervals up the wall. Alternatively, you could use a spirit level.

Dragging a wall

Dragging is most effective when darker glazes are used over a paler background and when the shades used are noticeably different; for example, magnolia glaze dragged over a white base will not show at all. Likewise, white dragged over pink shows much less than pink dragged over white. The color of your top glaze (the dragging) will come across as the main color in the room. Here, fresh yellow is dragged over a white background making the room look yellow, even though the base color is pure white.

EXPERT TIPS

- *If your glaze is too thin you will find that the stripes you make with the dragging brush fade away in a few seconds. This is easy to remedy by thickening the glaze a little. Add about half a cup more paint and half a cup more glaze to the mix. If you don't have any paint or glaze left, leave the existing batch to evaporate overnight in a well-ventilated area.*

- *Glaze which is too thick results in uneven strokes and stripes which do not run all the way from ceiling to floor; thin the glaze by adding a few splashes of mineral spirits at a time and stirring well. Do not be tempted to add a lot of thinners in one go—it is easy to over-dilute glaze.*

- *If the glaze is not dark enough, and there is no contrast between the back-ground color and the stripes, mix a teaspoon of artist's color into a small amount of the glaze, add this to the paint kettle and stir well.*

1 To make the glaze, mix together the alkyd-based scumble glaze and the alkyd-based paint, then add enough mineral spirits to thin the mixture to the consistency of evaporated milk. Using a large household brush, brush the glaze down the wall with vertical strokes. Apply the glaze evenly so that both edges are straight.

2 Immediately take a dragging brush and position it at the top of the wall so that the bristles and handle are vertical. Press the brush into the wet glaze so that it bends or flexes at the point where the bristles meet the handle and all of the bristles are in contact with the glaze. Holding this position, pull the brush all the way down the wall in one even stroke. The brush will produce fine stripes as it moves through the glaze. The pattern is formed at the point where the bristles meet the brush; the rest of the long hairs feather and soften the stripes.

3 For very high rooms, a good trick is to use a very soft household broom taped on the end of a long pole and work from the floor, stepping backwards as you pull the broom down the wall.

Other paint effects

MATERIALS

FOR THE GLAZE
- 1 liter (32 fl oz) scumble glaze
- 1 liter (32 fl oz) paint
- paint kettle or bucket
- household brush
- mineral spirits or water

TOOLS FOR EFFECTS
- stippling brush
- cotton rag, 40 cm (16 in) square
- plastic carrier bags
- natural sea sponge
- brown paper or newspaper

The dragging technique shown on page 36 is one of many paint effects which you can create using the same ingredients. Paint effects are created by moving a slippery, colored glaze around on a painted surface and then leaving it to dry. Different effects are created by varying the tool used to move the glaze. You can work with either water-based or alkyd-based products. Water-based glazes dry faster than oils but have less shine. Alkyd-based glazes may last longer, but beware of blues in oil, as they will go yellow behind pictures and in dark areas as time goes by. Exposing a yellowing patch to the light will eventually bring the color back.

Glaze techniques need to be carried out on a mid sheen base coat, such as low sheen or satin. Flat paint is not a suitable base for glazing over.

MIXING GLAZE

Mix together in a paint kettle or bucket equal quantities of scumble glaze and paint in your chosen color; 1 liter (32 fl oz) of each will be sufficient for a room the size featured on page 34. Use alkyd-based (satin) paint with alkyd-based glaze, and low sheen paint with water-based scumble glaze. Mix thoroughly with a household brush and dilute with mineral spirits or water, as appropriate, until the mixture is about the thickness of cream. If you put some of this mixture on to your hands, you will notice its slippery feel, rather like cooking oil.

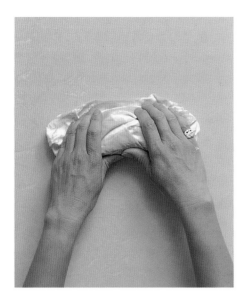

RAG ROLLING

Using a household brush, apply some glaze to the wall over an area about 1 m (40 in) square. To achieve a professional finish, stipple away all the brushstrokes by jabbing the surface of the wet glaze lightly with a large brush (see Stippling, page 38); using a stippling brush saves time and energy as it has a larger surface area than a household brush. Then scrumple a cotton rag up in your hand. Keep all the tatty edges and seams tucked away. Gently roll the rag up the wall, in any direction. The dry rag will lift the glaze away from the wall and produce a random pattern.

RAGGING

Ragging is a much more subtle paint effect than rag rolling; it has more of a marbled look and is easy to do. Apply the glaze as before, working in areas about 1 m (40 in) square. Now gently dab a crumpled rag over the wet surface of the glaze. The more you dab, the flatter the final effect will be. Cotton sheeting is best if you are looking for a smooth ragging. Obviously, you must avoid lint in the cloths, so yellow dusters cannot be used for ragging.

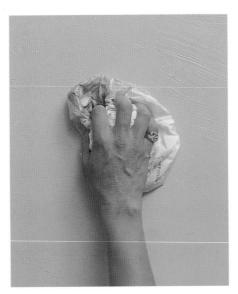

COLORWASHING

This paint effect is very simple to do. Dip a soft cotton rag into the glaze and wring it out. Then wipe the wall with the wet rag in any direction you choose, in the same way you would if you were washing the walls with soap and water. The more you rub the paint into the wall, the more delicate the finish will be.

Work with a fairly thin glaze, the consistency of milk, in sections as large as you can safely reach to cover.

For an aged effect, apply a second coat in a curve around the top and bottom corners and around the ceiling join, rather like a misted picture frame. This second coat is fast to apply and gives a professional edge to the work.

BAGGING

This effect looks like old leather. A thicker glaze is best for bagging. Make up the glaze as on page 38 but without mineral spirits or water so that the glaze is the consistency of hair shampoo. Apply the glaze quite thickly over an area about 1 m (40 in) square using a household brush; there is no need to remove the brushstrokes. Turn a plastic carrier bag inside out (to prevent the printing ink mixing with the paint) and crumple it up in your hand. Dab the crumpled bag all over the wet sticky glaze. Thicker bags make a more dramatic effect; try a few before deciding which one to use and make sure you have several of the same type to get you around the entire room.

SPONGING

One-color sponging tends to be overused by decorators; however, two-color sponging is very effective. You do not need a glaze for sponging; you can use any paint, directly from the can. Always use a natural sea sponge and try to find one that looks a bit hairy, with tiny spikes. Soften the sponge in water or mineral spirits before using it, then wring it out. Dip the sponge very lightly into a shallow tray of paint (the lid of the can will be fine). Dab the sponge lightly on to a piece of newspaper or cloth to remove the excess paint, then dab it very lightly all over the wall. Move your hand around into different positions as you go to avoid repeat marks. Use a tiny piece of sponge for tricky areas such as edges.

When you have covered the whole wall, repeat the process with the next color. Sponging the lightest color first works best; this produces an effect of shading. Always work lightly as heavy pressure will reveal the marks of the holes in the sponge rather than creating a soft speckled effect.

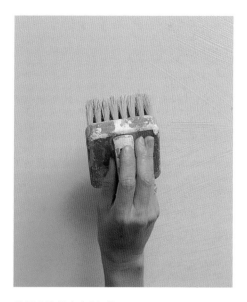

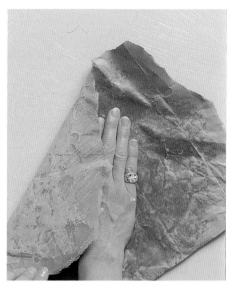

STIPPLING

Stippling is considered to be one of the most difficult paint effects to execute perfectly. However, the result is elegant and well worth doing. Work with a thick glaze as for bagging and apply the glaze in 1 m (40 in) square sections. Jab a stippling brush over the wet surface, revealing tiny pin-prick marks, barely visible and just slightly textured. Concentrate on creating an even finish; stippling in its purest form should not look like clouds. Use the brush to move paint from darker patches by jabbing it into the patch and then on to a dry area of the wall. For a transparent effect, use alkyd-based glaze with just a touch of color.

FROTTAGE

This paint effect is messy, quick and fun to do. Frottage produces a very random, mottled effect, rather like the look of old plaster. Working with a thin glaze and using more than one color can be effective, as can working with newspaper, which leaves touches of printing ink in the finished effect as a dirty tint. Experiment on a piece of white hardboard until you arrive at the effect you like.

Apply the glaze in 1 m (40 in) square areas with a household brush, then immediately press a piece of brown paper or newspaper on to the wet glaze. Pull it off straight away to reveal the effect. The same piece of paper can be re-used several times before it becomes too wet to absorb any more of the glaze.

An abundance of pure white, brought to life with splashes of ultramarine blue, will create a fresh and imaginative room scheme.

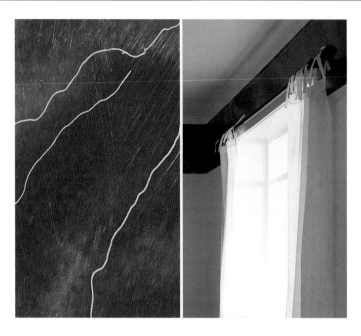

Clean White

Pure, clean, crisp, fresh, cool and unimposing: white is all of these. Unfortunately, it can also be described as boring, unimaginative, plain and lack-luster. This stunning room makes use of white, white and more white, all brought to life with a single crafty accent color, ultramarine blue.

Contrary to popular opinion, white does not make a room look larger. Nor does it make a room look any lighter than say, pale yellow or blue. White is cooling, however, and you must consider

PROJECTS FROM
THIS MAKEOVER
SHOW YOU:

• *How to choose an accent
color*

• *How to paint a door*

• *How to paint a marbled
strip*

• *How to dry-brush a
wooden floor*

45

this if you are working in a cold room. Bear in mind also that evening lighting may yellow the overall effect unless you invest in low voltage halogen or daylight simulation bulbs.

The choice of ultramarine blue to accent the white prevents the room from seeming too cold. This strong color, which echoes the colors of an eggplant, adds a dramatic aspect.

The marbling technique seen around the top of the walls is simple to do and creates a softer effect than having plain painted cornices and dado rails. You can see the effect of horizontal stripes and observe how they draw your eyes along the walls, rather than up and down, thus reducing the impression of height.

CHOOSING AN ACCENT COLOR

There are no rules surrounding an accent color to go with a plain white room and you are at liberty to select your favorite. Any deep or intense tone will stand out from the white, whereas paler shades will not stand out so much. Using black with white is not recommended, however; the contrast between these two colors is true negative and may play tricks on your eyes in bright daylight. Instead, use a shade close to black, such as paynes gray which is a dark blue gray, almost black, or a very deep brown, such as vandyke brown. These two colors just take the edge off a pure black and are a little softer to live with.

If you are superstitious, avoid scarlet and white; it would be better instead to go for an indian red or alizarin crimson, both of which are deeper.

One way to choose an accent color is to consider the items you will be using in the room. One of these items will often dictate the color scheme to be used. If, however, you are starting from scratch, you can choose the color and then accessorize around it.

PAINTING A DOOR

Doors are subject to a high degree of wear and tear and a strong and durable paint, such as satin or gloss, is recommended for them; three coats will last for years. Paneled doors are very simple to paint section by section using the following method.

EXPERT TIPS

- *If you have left a drip in gloss paintwork, first let it dry. Then sand away the drip and re-paint the entire panel or section with a further coat of gloss paint.*

- *It is easier to work with several thin coats of gloss, rather than one thick coat which will be more likely to reveal brushstrokes and to drip or sag. Work slowly and very carefully; there is no speedy way to apply gloss paint.*

1 First paint the rebates or panels of the door; apply the paint evenly in an up-and-down direction.

2 Then paint the center vertical of the door, leaving the horizontal bar unpainted for the moment.

3 Paint the horizontals of the door: along the top, middle and bottom. Apply the paint in horizontal brush-strokes, leaving the sides of the door unpainted.

4 Finally, paint each side of the door from the top to the bottom with vertical brushstrokes. Follow the line of the rebates for a clean finish. Allow to dry.

Painting a marbled strip

MATERIALS
- 2 teacups alkyd-based scumble glaze
- 1 tbsp ultramarine blue artist's color
- 1 tbsp prussian blue artist's color
- 2 tsp driers
- household paintbrush
- badger softener
- hog's hair softener
- gold pen or fine artist's brush and gold paint

In this simple method of creating the effect of marble, pure artist's colors are mixed with a thick, oily glaze and blended in diagonal strokes until most of the brushstrokes disappear.

Marbling is a technique that each individual does differently. So if you are working with someone, you should ideally work together on the same areas with one person applying the glaze and the other softening. Otherwise, if you both marble a separate section of a surface you will be able to see clearly the two different styles of work when they finally meet up in the middle.

When you are working above eye level, as on this marbled strip, you do not need to concentrate too much energy on blending and smoothing as the fine details will not be visible to the naked eye from the ground. Step down from your ladder now and then and observe your work from the real viewing points.

1 Mix two shades of blue glaze, using 1 cup of alkyd-based scumble glaze and one of the artist's colors in each. Stir them both well and then add 1 teaspoon of driers to each glaze. Stipple or jab the glazes onto the cornice, using more of the prussian blue for a dark marble and more of the ultramarine blue if you are aiming for a brighter area. Bring the two colors right up against each other.

2 Working in sections about 1 m (40 in) square at a time, soften the wet glazes gently with a hog's hair softener. Stroke the wet glaze in a diagonal direction and gently blend the two shades of blue together. Most of the brushstrokes will still be visible at this point in the process.

3 Continue to brush the wet glaze in every direction to soften the brushstrokes using a badger softener. Wipe the brush clean regularly. If you are working at a height you do not need to obliterate all the brushstrokes as they will not be seen from ground level.

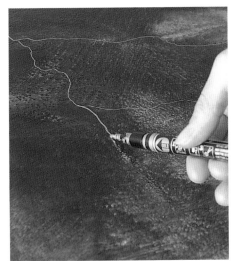

4 When the marble background is dry, draw or paint some fine gold veins across the surface using a gold pen or a fine artist's brush and gold paint. The veins should filter into each other. Avoid making crosses or right angles as these would not occur naturally in marble.

Dry-brushing a floor

MATERIALS
- household brush
- 1 liter (32 fl oz) alkyd-based paint in pale color
- 1 liter (32 fl oz) mineral spirits
- paint kettle or bucket
- large household brush

When this tongue and groove flooring was first laid, it was protected with clear varnish which allowed the natural beauty of the wood grain to shine through and reveal warm yellow or beachy tones. In this room it has been 'dry-brushed' with a pale color. Dry-brushing is a quick and inexpensive alternative to liming (where white paste is pushed into the grain of the wood and then polished). The pale paint does not actually sit deep in the grain of the wood but the effect is very similar to liming.

The paint will need to be protected from wear and tear after it has been applied; apply three thick coats of clear, floor-quality varnish. After you have finished, store any remaining paint.

As with all floor treatments, the best way to do them is barefoot and just before you leave the room for several hours.

1 Using a household brush and a paint kettle or bucket, mix together alkyd-based paint in your selected color and mineral spirits. The paint mix should be the consistency of milk. If you are using a gel-type paint, you may need to add a little more mineral spirits to achieve this required consistency.

2 Brush some of the paint on a spare piece of wood, or in a corner of the floor which is not easy to see, to test it. It should be slightly transparent, enabling the grain of the wood to be clearly visible through the paint.

E X P E R T   T I P S

- *Always varnish a painted floor to protect the paint. You can apply varnish to a floor in quick, fairly sloppy strokes as it will settle to a flat surface as it dries. Look out for flying splashes of varnish which may land on an area where the varnish is already beginning to dry; be sure to brush any of these out immediately.*

3 Using a large household brush, dip the edge of the bristles into the paint mix and wipe off any excess on the edge of the paint kettle. Begin painting at the point furthest away from the door, and work along the planks one by one, brushing the paint lightly along the grain. Complete the planks one at a time but do not paint yourself into a corner.

4 The paint may soak into the wood in places so, from time to time, stand back from your work and look for any areas that do not have sufficient color in them. Go over these areas with more paint, feathering the edges of the patches with a zigzag movement of the brush so that the new paint blends into the paint you have already applied.

*Use varying shades of neutral brown on both walls
and woodwork to create a warm and welcome room
with a relaxing ambience.*

Neutral Brown

Capitalizing on sunshine, this room in its shades of
neutral brown is warm and welcoming; you could
easily relax here with the Sunday papers.

Deep shades of neutral brown need a sunny or
light room to work well. A quick look at the area
of shade next to the window in the photograph
will show you the graying effect shadow can have.
While most of the photographs in this section
were taken at the same time of day, notice how
the floor reflects the tones of the walls and in this

PROJECTS FROM
THIS MAKEOVER
SHOW YOU:

• *How to mask off areas*

• *How to fill surface cracks
and holes*

• *How to colorwash a wall*

• *How to upholster a low
bench*

case has been toned down from a glowing cream to a beech tone. Artificial light is not a problem with neutrals and browns; ordinary light bulbs have a slight yellow tone to them which can enhance these colors.

The pinkish beige color above the picture rail was selected to echo the floor and furniture. Being paler than the colorwashed walls it 'lifts' the ceiling. The blue used on the ceiling is almost the opposite color to the beige above the picture rail and allows the introduction of blue accessories and fresher colors in the room. Careful selection of opposite colors for the area above the picture rail means that they counteract each other.

CHOOSING AN ACCENT COLOR

As colorwashing requires large sweeping strokes, you will need to remove or carefully mask off any areas that are not to be painted. Loosen the screws on light switches and plug sockets and carefully wrap the edges with masking tape. Use wide tape or newspaper to cover the remainder of the switch. For delicate areas, such as rails which are already painted, use a low-tack masking tape, which is not as sticky. You can reduce the tackiness of tape by pressing a new piece of tape on to a carpet or a rag before use. After applying paint, remove the masking tape while the paint is still wet. If you leave it to dry you will undoubtedly pull away some of the paint from the wall with the tape. To mask off carpets, apply the masking tape and then press it hard onto the carpet. Tuck the edge right under the skirting board.

PAINTING A DOOR

Many glazing techniques, such as colorwashing, need a perfectly smooth surface to be effective. Any cracks or imperfections will hold a thicker layer of glaze and this will show up clearly as a deeper colored patch in the finished surface. However, do not panic; filling cracks is an easy process and it takes very little time to do.

1 Using a filling knife, press some spackling compound into the crack, then carefully scrape away the excess. Always use flexible spackling compound if possible; it will expand and contract with the crack and last longer than non-flexible types.

2 Allow the spackling compound to dry and harden, then rub it down with medium-grade sandpaper to smooth the surface.

Colorwashing a wall

MATERIALS
- 500 ml (16 fl oz) alkyd-based paint
- 500 ml (16 fl oz) scumble glaze
- approx. 1 teacup mineral spirits
- household brush
- badger softener

Colorwashing is a term used so often to describe so many varied effects that it has almost become a generic term in the painting trade. It is actually a method for applying a thin glaze over the surface in such a way that the base color shows through a mottled surface. In this project the glaze is brushed on and spread out while it is still wet. A product known as scumble glaze is added to the paint to give it a slippery texture in order that the color will move about on the wall as you soften and spread it with the brush.

Colorwashing must be carried out on top of a base coat of low sheen or satin rather than flat paint. The slight sheen of the base coat is very important for the softening to be effective.

1 To make the colorwash glaze, mix the alkyd-based paint with transparent scumble glaze and stir well. Then add mineral spirits to thin the mixture until it is the consistency of cream.

2 Using a household brush, apply the glaze over the wall, working quickly in large criss-cross strokes, in sections about 1 m (40 in) square at a time. Leave some of the white base coat showing through between the brushstrokes and overlap many of the brushstrokes.

3 Spread the glaze with the same brush, in criss-cross directions, as far as it will easily go. This takes some physical energy but is very easy to carry out. Work fast and keep the edges of each section wet, overlapping each one as you go. Add more color if you want.

4 Without allowing the glaze to dry, sweep a badger softener all over the wet criss-cross marks in every direction. The soft floppy bristles of the badger brush will obliterate most of the visible brushstrokes, yet leave behind the variations of shade caused by the overlaps.

MATERIALS

- bench with cushion
- furniture fabric
- dressmaking scissors
- sewing machine
- matching thread
- drawing pins
- stapler and 6 mm (¼ in) staples
- calico, optional
- bradawl or skewer

Upholstering a bench

The blue bench featured in this room is upholstered in a thick weave linen fabric. The effect can easily be emulated by re-covering an old bench. If you have never attempted upholstery before, don't worry, it is not as difficult as you think.

The main point to remember is not to overtighten or overstretch the fabric as you pull it into place or the edges of the cushion pad will buckle. Use a thick fabric so that you can remove or reposition staples without tearing it.

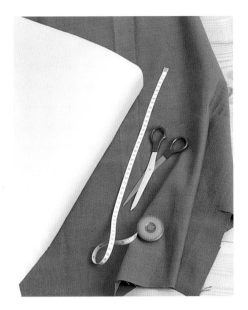

1 Remove the bench legs. Cut a piece of furniture fabric to fit all around the bench seat with a 5 cm (2 in) overlap on each side for the staples. In this case a rectangle was all that was required. Oversew the edges of the fabric using a sewing machine and machine thread to prevent them from fraying; this is particularly important with coarse weave fabrics which tend to fray easily.

2 Stretch the fabric around the bench and hold it in place on the underside with drawing pins. Fold the corners down neatly and secure these with pins too.

3 While removing the drawing pins one by one, stretch the fabric over the seat, securing it on the underside with staples. Try to keep an even tension as you pull the fabric or the cushion pad will begin to undulate.

E X P E R T   T I P S

- *For those feeling more adventurous, fabric can be painted or embroidered for the bench. Commercially available fabric paints are durable through many washes but will not stand scrubbing so you will have to remove the cover regularly for washing. For appliqué applications, the amount of stretch in the appliqué must be the same as in the main piece of fabric or the stitches will tear and the fabric will not sit evenly when it is stretched on the bench.*

4 Hide any rough edges on the base with a piece of spare matching fabric or calico. Staple this fabric to the base. You may need to trim the first piece of fabric at the corners to avoid bulging.

5 Once the upholstery is complete, re-attach the legs of the bench. Use a bradawl or kitchen skewer to locate the holes, then screw the legs into place through the layers of fabric.

MAKEOVER PROJECT

The crisp cleanliness of magnolia and cream tones can be used to create a bright and classical atmosphere in your living room.

Classical Cream

Dispelling the myth that plain magnolia means nothing without color, flavor or imagination, this room uses the crisp cleanliness of magnolia tones and cream paints to produce a bright and classical atmosphere which was initially inspired by some of the work of the architect Robert Adam.

With a pale floor and walls, the eye is drawn to the deepest tones in the room; here these are the ageing on the border and the coach lining. A dark floor would also work well in this room and is

PROJECTS FROM
THIS MAKEOVER
SHOW YOU:

• *How to strip old paint*

• *How to mix an ageing glaze*

• *How to age a border*

• *How to paint a faux stone pot*

worth considering if your room is cool. This would draw the eye down and create a balance against the border. If your room is already painted with cream or magnolia paints you will be able to begin with the border and careful accessorizing to create this look.

The floor in this room has been dry-brushed with off-white paint and varnished with three coats of polyurethane gloss. Each coat of varnish takes about half an hour to apply and is left to dry overnight. Polyurethane varnish is very tough and hardwearing. It will protect the paint finish for at least a year before it requires a further coat or two.

STRIPPING OLD PAINT

If your existing woodwork has been painted many times, you may have lost some of the definition in the carving. To strip old paint, and renew the shape of rails or carved details, apply a gel stripper to the painted surface by jabbing it on liberally with an old brush. Take care not to brush the stripper on as this neutralizes the chemicals. Once the gel has been jabbed on to the paint it will start to bubble. Remove the gel and old paint with a scraper; use an old toothbrush for intricate areas. If the paint does not come away easily, wait for a couple of minutes or apply another layer of gel stripper. When you have removed all the old paint, wash the wood with mineral spirits to neutralize fully any remaining gel stripper.

MIXING AN AGEING GLAZE

It is possible to make a surface look old and time-worn without having to wait for this to occur by itself. In this room the border has been aged with a simple glaze technique, using a deeper and more yellow tone than that used on the walls. Keeping to yellower, deeper tones not only provides harmony in the color scheme but actually produces the same effect as real ageing. Most paints tend to yellow with age so white becomes yellow, pink becomes beige and blue becomes more greenish. Mixing a drop of yellow ochre into the color you use will help you to find a natural aged tone.

1 Mix together a tablespoon each of yellow ochre and raw umber artist's oil colors with about half a cup of mineral spirits in a small pot. Stir the mixture thoroughly until all the lumps have dispersed. Add more mineral spirits if necessary until you have a thin watery mix.

2 Pour the diluted oil paints into about 500 ml (16 fl oz) of transparent, alkyd-based scumble glaze and stir well. The glaze should be the same consistency as cream.

- decorative border
- satin alkyd-based paint
- household brush
- ageing glaze
- cloth
- 1 tbsp yellow ochre artist's oil color
- 1 tbsp raw umber artist's oil color
- approx ½ teacup mineral spirits
- fine artist's brush
- rag

Ageing the border

The ornate border was ordered through a wallpaper supplier. It looks like flooring material and is very heavy to work with; it is actually made from linseed oil. Borders like this were traditionally used in stately homes and will last for 200 years or more. Allow the recommended paste to soak into the border for a couple of minutes before applying it; wipe away any excess glue with a damp rag. After pasting the strips of border, loop them into manageable sections to make it easier to carry them up the ladder. It doesn't matter if you get paste on to the good side of the border as it can easily be wiped away with a damp cloth. When applying the border to the wall, use the cornice as a guideline and butt the border up against it as you slide it into position.

Ageing must be carried out on a surface that has a slight sheen to it. The border in this room was first painted with two coats of alkyd-based paint in pale cream.

1 After painting the border with velvet paint, in this case the same color as the ceiling, allow it to dry. Then, using a household brush, apply the ageing glaze (see page 63) in large criss-cross strokes, working in sections about 1 m (40 in) long. Make sure you push the glaze well into the moldings of the border with the bristles of the brush.

2 While the glaze is still wet, fold a cloth to form a pad and wipe this over the wet glaze. Most of the glaze will come away on to the cloth, leaving behind only a trace of color on flat areas of the border and more defined staining in the crevices. Continue applying and wiping the glaze until you reach a corner. Any delay causes the glaze to dry and leave a mark where you start the next section.

3 For the coach lining, mix together the yellow ochre and raw umber artist's oil colors then dilute with mineral spirits to a watery consistency. Using a fine artist's brush apply the color into the carved lines on the picture rail, painting right into the grooves.

4 While the brown paint is still wet, wipe away any excess using a rag dampened with mineral spirits and wrapped around your finger or thumb. Run the rag along the edge of the groove to make clean, straight lines. Use clean sections of the rag for each wipe.

MATERIALS

- plastic pot
- wire brush or coarse-grade sandpaper
- household brushes
- white primer for glossy surfaces
- cream textured masonry paint
- sand, optional
- beige textured masonry paint
- cloth
- rottenstone powder, optional

Painting faux stone

The plant pot shown here has the look and feel of stone. But, if you pick it up you will soon realize that it is feather-light and has never seen a quarry or a stone mill. The pot is in fact a very inexpensive plastic urn bought from a garden center. This was then transformed with the aid of a few coats of cream and beige masonry paint which were dabbed and rubbed in with a brush and cloth.

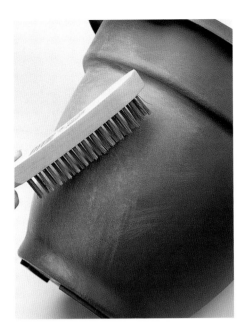

1 Rub the surface of a plastic pot with a firm wire brush or coarse-grade sandpaper until it is rough. This creates a 'key' for paint to adhere to; paint would simply peel off a smooth plastic surface.

2 Using a household brush, prime the outside of the pot with a coat of white primer for glossy surfaces. Allow the paint to dry fully before moving on to the next step.

3 Paint the pot with at least two coats of cream masonry paint, allowing each coat to dry before applying the next; this paint has sand mixed into it at the manufacturing stage and it feels rough to the touch when dry. If desired, you can add extra sand to the paint before applying it for a rougher finish.

4 Paint around the moldings at the top and bottom of the pot with beige masonry paint to add shading. Dab the paint on roughly and rub it while wet with a cloth. Alternatively, you could rub rottenstone powder (gray pigment made from ground stone) into the cream masonry paint before it dries.

Use varying shades of pale blue to create a fun play area for children by day and a relaxing haven for stressed adults by night.

Bleached Blue

Sometimes the compromise forced upon you when deciding how to decorate a room is great; probably none greater than a room that serves adult purposes such as relaxation in the evening and the complete opposite during the day: kids! This room uses pale blues and fun stripes, all fully washable. The striking rug hides the ultimate in dual-purpose—a painted play area to keep the children amused in their world of fantasies.

Blue is a cool color, particularly if the room faces

PROJECTS FROM
THIS MAKEOVER
SHOW YOU:

• *How to choose safe paints for children*

• *How to paint stripes with a roller*

• *How to make a one-off stencil*

• *How to corrode a tin bucket*

away from the sun. Its opposite color is yellow, which can be used to neutralize the effect. In a very shady room, blue can look gray and feel cold so be careful when choosing shades of blue and keep the color bright and cheery. The crisp blues used in this room were selected using shades from the same card in the paint store.

The striped effect is created using a foam roller and a ball of string, a simple and speedy technique which takes half an hour to do. The play mat takes longer but is fun to paint. One advantage of painting for children is that they are less critical of your work than adults. You are not expected to turn out a masterpiece!

SAFE PAINTS FOR CHILDREN

Some paints may still contain toxic elements. Always check the can for full information and look out for any warnings on labels. Paints that advertize their 'traditional' manufacture are likely candidates for a toxic ingredient, such as lead. Paints that have been developed for use in restoration, for historic houses and in association with the owners of heritage buildings, are even more likely to be unsuitable for use around children. It is therefore recommended to confine your paint choice to good all-round products that are sold in thousands of liter quantities each week and manufactured in the most basic fashion. The big names in paint do not add any lead to their products, even though there may be a trace. They also use stainers that are considered safe and non-toxic.

PAINTING BASIC STRIPES

Basic stripes applied with a paint roller are quick to create; this room took only 20 minutes to stripe. Rollered stripes have soft blurred edges caused by the foam expanding and contracting as the pressure you exert changes.

If you want tiny stripes, a small foam roller will be most suitable. However, a small roller will hold less paint and may not get you all the way down the wall in one sweep. Decide how to overlap with a newly loaded roller; using a paper or painted border to cover the overlap may be suitable.

1 Wrap string, ribbon or elastic bands tightly around both ends of a paint roller, as shown here. The more sponge you can still see, the wider the stripes you will paint on the wall.

2 Using a paint tray with about 1 cm (½ in) depth of paint in the reservoir, dip the roller in the tray and load it evenly all round. Test the painted pattern on a piece of paper and practice painting an even stripe before starting.

3 Attach a plumbline to the wall to act as a guideline. Apply the striped pattern on the wall, re-loading the roller with paint after each stroke. When dry, brush a coat of emulsion glaze over the top for a washable surface.

Making a one-off stencil

MATERIALS
- design for stencil
- hard pencil
- good-quality tracing paper
- scalpel or craft knife
- masking tape or spray mount
- paintbrush or sponge
- water-based paint

If you are not confident of your painting capabilities and are afraid to paint freehand, using a stencil will help you enormously. Most of the stencilled designs on this floor were painted only once, so a long-lasting stencil was not required; disposable paper ones were made for the lettering and teddies.

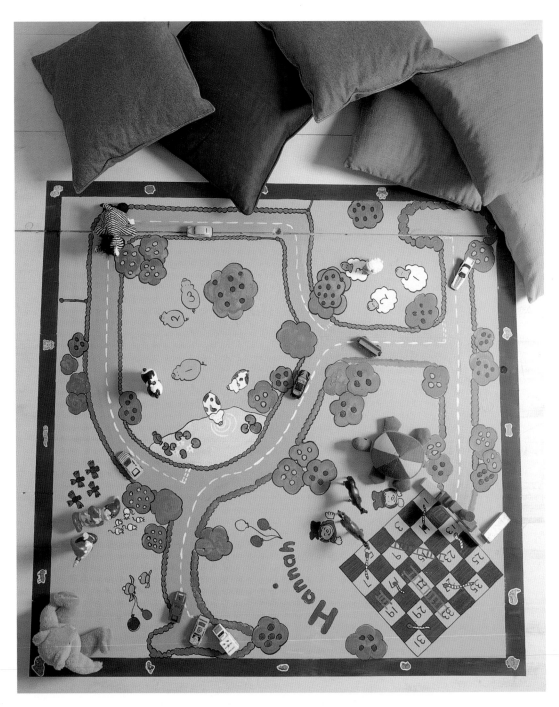

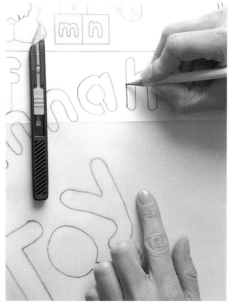

1 Find a design you would like to use for a stencil. Using a photocopier, enlarge it until it is the size you need. These images came from children's activity and coloring books.

2 Using a hard pencil, trace the enlarged design carefully on to a sheet of good-quality tracing paper, which is readily available from art shops. Check that you have traced the whole design.

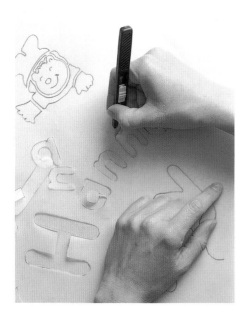

3 Using a scalpel or craft knife, cut out the design, leaving a gap between sections that will be painted in different colors, such as the sweaters and trousers on the teddies.

4 Position the stencil on the floor and secure with masking tape or spray mount. Then load a brush or sponge sparingly with water-based paint and carefully dab the color through the cut stencil. Lift away the stencil carefully as soon as you have applied the color and leave the design to dry.

Corroding a tin bucket

MATERIALS
- rubber gloves
- goggles
- face mask
- tin or untreated metal bucket
- steel wool or wire brush
- corroding chemical
- old paintbrush
- spray lacquer or acrylic clear varnish

The tin bucket in this room was purchased bright and shiny from a street vendor in South Africa. Tin items are widely available around the world. Some are available corroded, some will rust or corrode in time and some, like this one, can be encouraged to age with a chemical process.

There is a variety of chemicals that can be used to corrode metal, some of which are noxious and must be treated with respect. Always test on a tiny area first as chemical reactions can be unpredictable. Remember always to work in a well-ventilated area or outdoors, and always have the correct neutralizing agent at the ready; this is normally a bucket of water or a garden hose. For protection, wear gloves, goggles and a face mask when dealing with corroding chemicals.

1 Wearing rubber gloves, goggles and a protective face mask, rub down the tin bucket with steel wool or a wire brush to remove any lacquer or finish applied in the factory.

2 Paint or rub the corroding chemical on to the metal, taking care not to drip or splash on to any areas not to be treated. Corroding metal just around the edges, where metal will age naturally, is very effective. The reaction should be immediate but wait a while for it to finish.

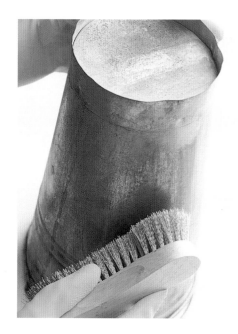

3 Allow the corroded bucket to dry fully, when the chemicals may cause it to look a little dusty. Rub the bucket down again with a wire brush or steel wool which will reveal some of the original shine.

4 Spray the bucket with a coat of clear spray lacquer or acrylic varnish to prevent rust forming, and allow to dry.

EXPERT TIP

- *Corroding chemicals can also be used on surfaces that have been gilded. However, be careful when using steel wool as this will not only remove the corrosion but the gold leaf as well. The following chemicals are available through any gold leaf supplier.*
  CAUSTIC SODA – This will corrode and blacken any untreated metals. It does not work on stainless steel or highly polished metals.
  AMMONIUM CHLORIDE AND COPPER SULPHATE – These are sold ready mixed as 'instant rust' which creates real rust when applied to raw iron or steel. The rust develops for several days afterwards.
  SODIUM SILICATE AND IRON OXIDE – These blacken any verdigris or rust finish as a second application. This is sold ready mixed as a blackening tint and is easy to use.
  CUPRA – This green liquid corrodes any metal with copper in the alloy to create green verdigris.

DINING ROOM MAKEOVERS

For many people, mealtimes are social events, often providing an opportunity to retreat from the busy world and catch up on each others' lives. It is therefore not surprising that food preparation, and the environment in which we eat food, are becoming an art form, attracting the world's leading designers and fashion gurus. People have started to realize that, for many of us, dining goes hand in hand with relaxation, so creating a stylish, comfortable eating environment should be of the upmost importance.

Yet, you do not need to be an interior designer to create a sumptuous dining area. The most interesting of effects can be achieved with a little experimentation. As this section demonstrates, the same room can be completely transformed simply by playing with color and texture. Using a range of decorative techniques, together with a series of color themes, this section should provide plenty of easy-to-follow, inspirational ideas for both beginners and more advanced decorators.

Striking primary colors as well as softer, earthy and metallic hues, can all be used to dramatic effect in creating a unique dining room. Each makeover in this section demonstrates how the same space can be transformed beyond recognition, simply by using different decorative techniques. From the chic style of metallic silver, to a countryside green and yellow, the rich spiciness of deep red or the dramatic impact of ultramarine, each transformation adopts its own striking style. While many restaurant

designers follow convention in choosing dining room colors – green is popular because it is associated with hunger, pale blue is said to suppress appetite – the projects in this section show that dining room colors can be as fun and wild as you like, and that anything, quite literally, goes.

Dining rooms must also be practical rooms, often accommodating a range of different functions. The white and primary room demonstrates that space restriction needn't affect style, offering practical hints for creating a room that can be easily transformed from working office to relaxing dining environment in a matter of moments. There are also practical points for storage solutions, and a range of quick, simple projects that can give your room that finishing touch.

Exploring the role of color and the different effects of light and space, this section goes on to examine the practical issues of choosing the correct tools and equipment for creating a paint effect. Each makeover also provides basic advice on preparation

and techniques, as well as step-by-step advice for completing decorative projects. Everything you need to know, including a few hints, tips and various tricks for creating the dining room you've always dreamed of, are included in these pages.

If you are nervous about using strong colors, try positioning painted boards in the dining room for a few days, to see how the color reacts in different light conditions. A room that is used for both sunny breakfasts and low-lit evening meals should be comfortable, offering the right sense of atmosphere, whatever the occasion.

The ideas presented in this section are not meant to be exhaustive. Designed partly for the beginner, they can be followed step-by-step to transform an entire room, or they can be borrowed as sources of inspiration for other, more original transformations.

Both decorating and dining should be a source of rewarding pleasure. Where better to begin than by redecorating your dining room?

Using color in your dining room

Color can transform a room dramatically. It can create the impression of height or receding walls, it can make a room feel cosy and intimate or airy and spacious, and it can form an independent style with an individual atmosphere. Dining rooms need to be comfortable and sociable, as well as practical and easy to maintain, so think about the effect you want to achieve before choosing the final color scheme.

CHOOSING COLORS FOR SPACE AND TEMPERATURE

Two primary ways in which color affects the environment lie in feelings of temperature and space. Some colors can create the sense of a large, airy room or a small, confined area, while others seem to suggest warmth and heat, regardless of the actual temperature. Identifying the colors to create these effects is not difficult. Red and orange are the colors of fire, and it therefore follows that red tones, or the use of red in a paint mix, will create a sense of warmth. Ice is bluey gray in color, and such paint tones also have a cooling effect. Interestingly, red and blue mixed together create purple, which can be deep and warming, or quite harsh, depending on the ratio of colors.

However, white can be hot (white heat) or cold (white ice). In fact, when a color wheel, comprising all of the colors in the spectrum, is spun at great speed the color seen is white. White

Dining rooms should be comfortable, stylish and welcoming. Keep the room versatile by using a diverse range of color and texture combinations, but remember that the aim should always be to create an inviting, relaxing environment. Think about the light, space and specific functions of your dining room, before deciding on a final color scheme.

will cool or warm, depending upon the lighting and the accessories used in the room. It takes its cue from the colors it is reflecting. The white room featured on page 108, for example, appears cool during daylight when it is used as an office and warmer in artificial evening light, which tends be quite yellowing.

For space, think of the blues and pale colors associated with the sky, the browny yellows of desert expanses and the greens of rolling hills. All of these colors evoke feelings of space and recede to make a room look just a little larger than it really is. For cosy environments, think about how dark colors, particularly reds, deep browns or maybe even blacks suggest warmth and confinement. Just as dusk and sunset anticipate the end of the day, so red and dark tones tend to advance and close in on us, reducing the sense of space.

CEILING COLORS
The ceilings were deliberately kept pale in all of the rooms featured in these pages. They are not all white however; pale yellow is used in the yellow and green room and beige is used in the copper and red rooms. Pale ceilings increase the feeling of height, perhaps because the colors convey a sense of the sky as the eye is drawn upwards.

To gauge the effect of different potential colors, try cutting out some colored paper or tinted plastic and positioning it on the ceiling of the room featured in this section. Some shades work better than others,

but the procedure can be useful for identifying how different potential combinations might work.

It's worth bearing in mind that some deeply colored ceilings can look cheap and unfinished. As a general observation, if the color selected for the ceiling is brighter or more vivid than that used on the walls it will be caught in your vision at all times and may detract attention from the wall colors and finishes.

Remember also, that dark ceilings will not reflect light back down into the room as effectively as pale ones. This can have the effect of lowering the height of the dining room, particularly if there are additional horizontal features, such as the checkered paint effect walls on page 134. A safe bet when painting a ceiling is to use the same color as the walls, with some white mixed in to make it a few notes paler. This is also an economical method for using leftover wall paint.

DIVIDING COLOR

Using different colors on walls in the same room can be tremendously effective. Whether you paint each wall a different hue, or

go for matching opposite walls, the effect should be quite striking. Perhaps try varying tones of the same color, for example the top and bottom shades from a paint sample card, to enhance shadows and define some of the architectural features of the room. Complementary colors – those opposite each other on the color spectrum such as red and green or yellow and purple – can also create stunning effects.

The room used for the makeovers in this section has neither a picture or dado rail. However, such wall features can make useful divisions for color although, like horizontal stripes, they do tend to bring down the height of the room. This is because horizontal features encourage the eye to move around – rather than up and down – the walls, thus giving the impression of width rather than height. Conversely, vertical stripes or vertical divisions in color, such as those used in the red and orange room on page 116, tend to raise the ceiling, particularly if it is painted in a pale color.

MIXING COLORS

Toning down or adjusting colors needn't mean investing in separate pots of paint. In fact, the hue of many paints can be adjusted with the use of stainers or artists' tubes of paint. When having paint mixed for you in a DIY store, keep a keen eye on the stainers as they squirt into the can. These are the basic colors in the mix and the addition of any one in a small quantity will adjust the shade of

83

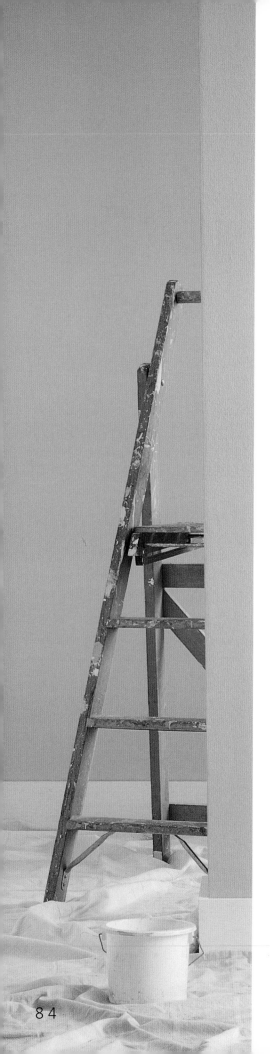

the paint without taking it too far from its color family. There is always one, predominant color in any mix and many paint codes reveal this information in the numbers and letters they use. Once you have established what colors are added to a professional mix, why not try experimenting yourself by investing in some similar colors?

Raw umber, a dark mucky brown is the most common color for 'knocking back' or dulling a color. It is very powerful so use it sparingly and bear in mind that the paint will dry a little darker than it looks when wet. For brightening try yellow or red, depending on the original color. White makes a paint paler although, interestingly, black is seldom used to darken colors as it has a dramatic graying effect.

Paint suppliers have a huge range of potential colors and mixes that they can get in stock. However, nothing beats practice, experimentation and experience. Mixing your own colors can help to create an individual look and helps to make the whole process of decorating and DIY feel so much more personal.

MUTED COLORS

Natural beiges, grayish greens and other muted colors are an excellent starting point for anyone who is daunted by the idea of introducing a new color scheme to a room. Readily available in a range of shades, these colors were inspired by historic buildings and the quest to discover how paints were mixed in years gone by. Of course, muted colors are now made

MUTED
Gray

Just as white paint now comes in a variety of off-shade colors, so gray needn't be a straightforward mix of black and white. Adding a hint of green, blue or even purple, can turn a basic gray mix into something a little more sophisticated and stylish. Muted grays are particularly popular as backgrounds for striking accessories or decorations such as pictures.

SUNSHINE
Yellow

Automatically associated with sunshine, yellow evokes feelings of cheerfulness wherever it is used. It is a popular choice for people making their first step away from safe magnolia, although intensive yellow, such as sunflower, can be too strong for small rooms. Choose buttery yellows for a soft effect or orangey yellows for a golden, vibrant feel.

without the addition of toxic ingredients, but the color representation is just as good as the original versions. Generally speaking, muted colors bring a relaxed air to the room, creating a gentle and subtle environment. They make excellent backgrounds for displaying special accessories such as new furniture or curtains.

EFFECTIVE LIGHTING

Light has a dramatic effect on color, particularly the range of natural light intensity that occurs throughout the day. Light can cause shadows and natural highlights, it can soften harsh colors or work with strong colors to create bright, vibrant environments. Ideally, dining rooms should be adaptable, providing the right atmosphere for morning coffee, leisurely family lunches and softly lit evening meals. The amount of natural light available at these times of day will obviously vary, so it is useful to think about how your chosen color will react in different forms of controlled lighting. For example, the bright, white and primary room on page 108 acquires a muted yellow effect with artificial evening light. Bear this transformation in mind when choosing a main, base color for the dining room. Artificial lighting, with the exception of daylight simulation bulbs, tends to make colors far more yellow and mellow than natural daylight. This is often a welcome evening transformation for most colors, but grays and pale blues can suffer, taking on a distinctly greenish hue.

Sometimes a change of lightbulb can make a vast difference to the feel of a room. Softly tinted lightbulbs, for example, can calm the harshest of tones, as can reducing the wattage of a bulb or using a dimmer switch. Candle light is always a warming and welcoming addition to any room, and is particularly useful for setting the atmosphere for a special dinner party or intimate meal. Experiment with large painted boards and different forms of lighting until you have found the perfect combination to suit your dining room.

TEXTURES IN DECORATION

Room makeovers need not be purely about color. Indeed, texture can be almost as dramatic as color, particularly in the way that different surfaces capture and reflect light. Different paint types, as well as actual surface variations, can create a combination of different decorative effects. For example, the corrugated card used in the stone and copper room (see p153), the leathery texture of the stripes in the red and orange room (see p144), and the remarkably flat finish achieved in the dramatic blue room (see p41), all demonstrate how texture can affect the feel of a room.

Similarly, the choice of fabric used in any accessories or upholstery will contribute to the general sense of the room. Natural, coarse weaves are less sumptuous than damasks or chenilles but they may complement the natural, stylish decor of the surrounding walls.

AQUA
Blue

Pale blues have a cooling effect on a room although vivid blues, those leaning towards turquoise or aqua, have some warming yellow in the mix, which tend to make them more welcoming. A very easy color to accessorize, blue harmonizes well with other tones of blue and all shades of yellow. This particular hue is brought to life with orange; effective if the furniture is made from aged pine or oregon wood.

EATING
Red

The most traditional dining color, eating red is very popular in established, high quality restaurants. Eating red has a hint of blue in it that tones down the usual advancing properties of brighter reds and will not make the room appear any smaller. Surprisingly, this deep tone can be used to brighten an environment, and works particularly well in softly lit areas, such as candlelight, helping to create a stylish ambience.

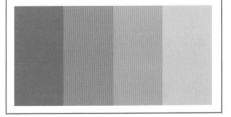

THE FUNCTIONAL CONSIDERATIONS

Dining areas must obviously be hygienic and easy to maintain. These factors should be taken into consideration when choosing the paint and accessories to decorate the room. For example, it's a good idea to make sure that any paint surfaces are washable and that upholstery can be easily removed and cleaned. Some effects, such as the textured walls in the stone and copper room (see page 124), are more vulnerable to damage than others and so are less suitable for busy family rooms than a sophisticated dining room used solely by adults. However, some treatments, such as the glaze effects in the red and orange room on page 116 and the green and yellow room on page 132, create a remarkably resistant surface and are ideal for busy family use. Keeping a small pot of spare paint to hand should also mean that a quick repair patch is exactly that – and doesn't get left to become a major redecorating mission.

FLOORS

It can be easy to ignore the floor when redecorating – it is, after all, the main surface from which you work and is therefore hardly the main focus of vision. Yet the floor can be as important to the overall feel and atmosphere of the decorated room as any other aspect of the scheme.

The potential expense of installing a new floor can be inhibiting so consider the possibility of using existing floor

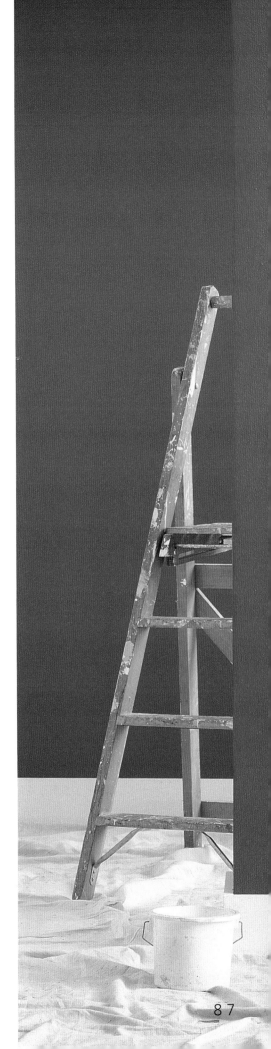

boards. Sanded boards that are then stained or painted can look surprisingly good, even if a well-positioned rug is necessary for part of the surface. If it is not possible to change a carpet or floor, try to harmonize the decorating scheme with the existing floor. This does not necessarily mean that colors should match, indeed opposite colors such as turquoise and brown, or cream and navy, contrast well.

Remember that it can be a good idea to focus on the floor after wall or ceiling decoration, in order to avoid drips and spillages. However, bear in mind that major floor work can generate dirt and dust which will ruin wet paint surfaces. Using sanding tools along floor edges may also cause marks or scratches along skirting boards.

THE FINISHING TOUCHES

When using deep or bright colors for redecoration the quality of the finish is very important. Woodwork, such as door and window frames, skirting boards and architraves, must be finished to a neat, high standard to convey

ALMOST

Eggplant

Not quite burgundy and not quite eggplant, this deeply toned, reddish purple is perfect for rooms which have little natural light. It benefits from carefully positioned artificial lighting and brightly colored accessories that tend to come to life against such intense and deep tones. Gold and silver work particularly well against this color, enjoying the main focus of attention against the deep, warm and luxurious background.

HISTORIC
Green

Heritage colors are enjoying another popular revival. Most of them, like historic green, are muted shades of those seen in nature. They evoke a sense of the countryside and outdoors, and tend to have a pleasant cooling effect. Green is also associated with appetite and is popular in many commercial restaurants. It is a receding color, which means that it can make a room appear much larger than it actually is.

a sense of professionalism. For example, it can be common for gaps to develop between frames and walls as age causes surfaces to expand and move. Such problems can be easily remedied with spackling compound, applied with a specialist gun and rubbed smooth with the tip of a finger. Any other pits and holes should be rubbed smooth after filling, and all dust removed from the surface before painting begins. This will help to ensure that the final surface is as smooth and refined as possible.

Similarly, try to paint naturally straight lines. Although masking tape can help, do not rely on this to provide neat edges – paint can bleed under the tape and ruin the finish. Any paint that does stray should be removed immediately, or carefully scraped off of surfaces such as glass or tiles, once it is fully dry.

Take the time to clean and polish appropriate surfaces and touch-up any niggling little marks as soon as they occur. In the long run, this will help to keep maintenance work down, ensuring that the dining room looks as good as it first did, for much longer!

Simple and crisp, metallic colors bring a sense of serenity. Use these stylish shades for an uncluttered, elegant finish.

Chic Silver

Metallic colors are increasingly popular in every walk of life. Gold, copper, brass and silver are turning up everywhere, from fashion catwalks to the sleek homes of the rich and famous. Part of the attraction is their cool simplicity. Metallic colors have reflective qualities, creating spacious, stylish effects that are perfect for uncluttered home decor.

In order to maintain the full effect of pure silver, the accessories in this room were kept to

plain blacks, grays, creams and whites. However, a few touches of blue were added, which reflect attractively in the silver and create a soft pewter effect. The slate floor also has touches of colored pyrite in it, helping to create a striking contrast with the chic walls.

Although silver works well with most types of furniture, the simplicity of the accessories in this room help to maintain the crisp, uncluttered feel. Metallic colors should be allowed to revel in their own dynamic glory, so be bold and try to avoid concealing them with unnecessary decoration or clutter.

USING SPECIALIST PAINT

Although metallic paint is widely available in enamel form, it tends to be expensive and can be difficult to obtain in large quantities. One solution is to use paints that are made for film and theater sets. These paints are relatively cheap and come in a range of colors and quantities, although they are not designed to be hardwearing. However, by mixing the top coat with an acrylic stabilizer, the paint becomes much stronger and will be more resistant to knocks. This means the paint is ideal for use in rooms designed for sitting – such as a dining area – although it will still lack the strength necessary for a room that receives a lot of traffic, such as a hall.

Theater paints are made by mixing finely ground, pure pigments into an acrylic base and are sold by weight, rather than by volume.

HANGING LINING PAPER

Metallic paint tends to reveal lumps and cracks more acutely than normal emulsion, so it's important to ensure the walls are as smooth as possible. This may involve re-lining the wall surface. Lining paper can be hung vertically but, if wallpaper is likely to be applied at some later stage, hang it in horizontal strips. This will ensure the joins of the top paper do not align with those of the lining paper beneath.

1 Measure out the strips of lining paper so that they are just a few centimeters longer than the width of the wall to be covered. Cut straight from the roll, using a sharp pair of scissors or a craft knife.

2 Mix some wallpaper paste, following the manufacturer's instructions, and apply liberally over the lining paper. Make sure that the paste is applied evenly and that none of the edges are missed or left dry.

3 Gently fold the ends of the pasted strip into the middle of the piece, pasted sides together. Fold the piece further until it is a manageable size. Put the paper aside for the glue to soak in, and then paste the next piece.

4 Starting at either the top or the bottom of the room, apply the sheets of pasted paper to the wall and smooth with a large, flat brush. Press all the creases and bubbles out at the edges. Trim off the excess paper.

Using metallic wall paint

MATERIALS
- surface spackling compound
- abrasive papers
- metallic paint
- acrylic binder
- small household brush
- gloss roller and tray
- badger hair softener

Metallic paints are normally made by mixing finely ground metals into a paint base. However, the tiny metallic grains do not dissolve in the paint solution, rather they float and sometimes sink, collecting at the bottom of the paint tin. It is therefore essential to stir metallic paint regularly, so that the intensity of the shine does not increase as you approach the end of the paint. Metallic paint also needs to be applied with a little more care than ordinary emulsion. Overlaps of brush or roller marks cause fine lines, and these tend to create variance in the intensity of the metallic glow. However, the extra time and care involved in painting with metallic paints is definitely worth the effort. It probably took only an extra half hour to decorate this room with metallic paint, compared to using normal paints.

1 Fill any cracks or dents in the wall surface with an appropriate spackling compound before sanding down with medium, and then fine grade, abrasive papers. Unlike ordinary emulsion, metallic paint can not be used for filling small cracks so try to achieve a perfectly smooth finish before you begin painting.

2 Before beginning, test the paint for resistance and coverage by applying it to a discreet area of the wall. If the metallic paint does not adhere immediately, rub the wall lightly with fine grade wet-and-dry abrasive paper. This will help to give the surface a better grip, known as a 'key', for the paint.

3 After stirring the paint thoroughly, edge along the ceiling about 0.5m (20in) at a time. Do not be tempted to paint longer lengths – metallic paint must always be applied as wet paint to wet paint. So these edges should not have dried by the time the main surface area below has been covered.

4 Stir the paint again and apply generously to the surface, working up to the edged area. Then continue the edge (as in step 3). Stir the paint between each loading of a brush or roller and apply the paint generously with a brush, or for best results, with a roller designed for use with gloss paints, made of a fine furry pile.

5 As the wet paint is overlapped with the brush or roller, dark lines may start to appear. Soften these lines with a badger hair softener by squashing the bristles gently onto the surface and lightly rubbing the brush around in a circular motion. The hard edge between the strips should disappear.

6 Mix the top coat of theater paint with 25 per cent of an acrylic binder. (This should be available from the paint supplier.) The binder will help to make the paint more flexible and provides important protection from knocks and dirt. Apply this second coat using the same techniques as before.

Framing cutlery

MATERIALS

- ready-made box frame
- undercoat, paint and stain
- household paintbrush
- sheet of mount board
- ruler, craft knife, cutting board
- marker pens or crayons
- clips or eye rings
- screws and screw-driver
- cutlery
- glue

Kitchen implements make ideal decorative features for dining areas. Here, an elegant carving knife and fork, which don't get much use on a day-to-day basis, help add a finishing touch to the metallic silver of the room. The back of the boxed frame can be easily removed, so the cutlery is accessible for those few occasions when it is required. The clips are available from most DIY outlets, as are eye rings for fixing heavy or thick decorative items.

Before buying a box frame, think about the level of depth that is required – some boxes may be too shallow for the intended display items. Also, be sure to use clips that can be easily unfastened and that will not damage the card mount with regular usage. Remember that frames such as these are ideal for displaying almost any item. They are a particularly effective way of displaying collections of unusual small objects and antiques.

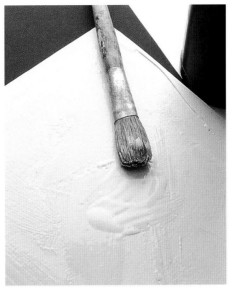

1 Paint the inside back section of the ready-made box frame with an appropriate undercoat and good quality wood paint. Apply at least two smooth coats of the final paint. This color will provide the contrasting border to the card mount.

2 Measure and cut the contrast square from thick framer's mount board. If the mount board shows a white card inner, color the edges with marker pens or crayons. Glue the contrast square onto the backboard of the box frame, using wood or contact adhesive.

3 Establish the exact positions of the items on the board and gauge where the clips will need to be. Then fix the clips or eye rings through the mount board and the back board of the box frame with screws. If necessary, use a tiny wedge of wood behind the card.

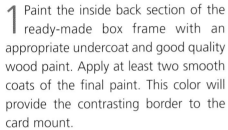

4 Treat any unstained or bare wood with woodstain or paint. Here, a black stain has been made by diluting some black artists' oil color with white spirit to a watery consistency. This provides a totally flat finish in one simple, quick drying coat.

5 Insert the board with the cutlery into the box frame and secure in place. Remember to make sure that the glass is spotlessly clean on both sides before repositioning it in the frame. Always take care when removing or repositioning the the framed cutlery and glass.

EXPERT TIP

- *Some ready-made box frames have a slide-in perspex cover, rather than glass. Although these do not tend to be as attractive as the glass versions, they are ideal for storing items that need to be removed quickly and regularly.*

Associated with the peace and tranquility of the sky and water, blue can also be bold, vibrant and remarkably strong.

Dramatic Blue

Rich, deep and eyecatching, blues such as ultramarine are commonly cited as favorite colors. They are popular choices for cars, clothes and pieces of furniture, yet strong blues tend to be neglected as potential colors for wall surfaces. This may be because strong, vibrant shades are often considered to be too bold or spirited for an actual living environment.

In fact, ultramarine is the perfect color for creating an active, stylish dining room. Its daring intensity reverses convention, forcing white to

PROJECTS FROM
THIS MAKEOVER
SHOW YOU

• *How to cut a stencil*

• *How to use different*
  stencilling methods

• *How to do reverse*
  stencilling

• *How to make foil*
  placemats

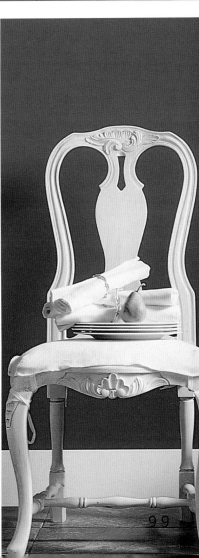

become an accent in the room, rather than the basic decorating staple. In fact, this role reversal of color can create some stunning results. The intensity of blue on the walls forces the lighter furniture and accessories to leap forward, producing a surprisingly sunny, vibrant feel. The simple reverse stencilling also helps to break up the drama, preventing the color from becoming too overpowering and helping to soften hard angles. The very flat theater paint used here helps to keep the texture velvety.

CHOOSING BOLD COLORS

Some rooms are naturally shady and may verge on being somber. Trying to brighten this kind of environment with white paint will only cause the reflection of shadows and create grayish hues. Sometimes a pale color, such as lemon yellow, may help but it can be more fun to try an intense, deep tone, such as the ultramarine blue used in this room. Other suitable colors include crimsons, terracottas and bottle greens. To understand how much a deep color can brighten a room, think about how strong colors are used to complement dark clothes. Crimsons, ultramarines and purples often seem much more vibrant when worn with darks or black.

Theater paints are made by mixing finely ground, pure pigments into an acrylic base and are sold by weight, rather than by volume.

CUTTING A STENCIL

Stencilling is an ancient technique that remains a popular form of decoration for both furniture and walls. It is simple to do, doesn't require any specialized equipment and can produce very stylish results. However, it's important to spend some time and thought over designing and making a stencil. Once the perfect pattern or shape has been created, the stencil can be used time and time again, providing a cheap and effective source for decorating walls and furniture.

1 Select a design that suits the room and will not lose any of its important details by being broken into sections. If the design is the wrong size, use a photocopier to enlarge or reduce the pattern and make a few spare copies for any later adaptations or unforeseen mistakes.

2 Stencil images are made up of different sections so study the design to see where filaments or breaks can be made. These should not interfere with the design, only help to break up the pattern into segments. Make marks on the shape to identify where the bridges will occur.

3 Draw or trace the design on to some plastic stencil sheets or stencil card. If it helps, shade in the areas that are to be cut out so that the bridges, and other areas that are to be left unpainted, are easy to identify. Remember to allow enough space around each shape for cutting out.

4 Cut out each section carefully with a sharp craft knife and use a cutting mat. Alternatively, use a stenciller's hot pen, which cuts through plastic quickly. Try to keep the edges of cuts as smooth and clean as possible, in order to avoid a scruffy edge on the paint finish.

MATERIALS
- artists' oil bar and palette
- stiff brush
- artists' acrylic/alkyd paints
- sponge
- paper
- colored glaze
- stippling brush

Stencilling methods

Hanging in the shelves at the front of this room is a little box frame which is a simplified version of the framing technique very popular in homes at the moment. This frame was quickly and easily made from an old sturdy box. Cigar boxes are ideal for this purpose. Some come branded with the cigar make and are attractive left unpainted.

SPRAY PAINTED

Spray paint tends to be very fine and travels into even the smallest of spaces so always ensure that the cut stencil adheres well to its chosen surface. Hold the nozzle at least 15cm (6in) away and spray in short bursts.

FEINT, OIL PAINTED

A popular method of stencilling, feint stencils are quick and easy to apply. Rub an artists' oil bar on to a palette and then swirl a short, stiff brush into the color. Apply through the stencil with a light, circular motion.

SPONGED

Either artists' acrylics, alkyds or emulsion paints can be used for this technique. Simply dip a section of dampened sponge into a small quantity of paint, dab off any excess and apply the paint with light jabbing motions.

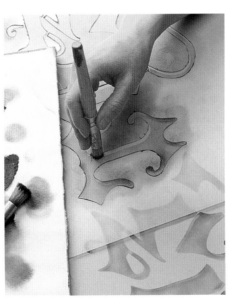

HIDDEN

This is the most subtle of the stencilling techniques. First, stipple the wall with a very lightly colored glaze, using the method shown on page 129. Once dry, apply the same glaze through the stencil. The stencilled effect is created by a double layer of stippled glaze.

SHADOWED

For a three dimensional effect, apply the stencil using one of the methods described above. Then remove the stencil and reapply it, about 2mm (¹⁄₁₆in) over the right or left hand edge. Color the border edges with a subtle shade, such as gray, to suggest the presence of a shadow.

Reverse stencilling

MATERIALS
- base paint
- plastic or card stencils/templates
- adhesive spray
- small household brush
- roller and tray
- 0.5 liter (17½ fl oz) of color paint

This simple technique does not require as much planning as the other stencilling methods and it is far less time consuming. This is because the design does not need to be given any connecting bridges; the images are, effectively, cut out silhouettes.

The technique of reverse stencilling is ideal for one-off projects, although the stencils can be reapplied. However, always make sure the back of each stencil is fully cleaned after use, to prevent any unwanted smudging.

1 Paint the chosen base color of the stencils onto the surface in the areas that the design is to appear. Use a roller to ensure that the patches of color are sufficiently large but do not worry about painting the whole wall at this stage.

2 Once dry, apply the stencils to the patches of color in their elected positions. Use adhesive spray on the back of each piece and press them fully into place. Work on half the wall at a time so that the stencils can be re-used elsewhere.

3 Gently stipple the final wall color around the edge of each stencil. This should help to prevent the paint from bleeding under the stencil when you come to use a roller for the rest of the room. Leave the stencils in place.

4 Paint the walls with a roller and fairly generous quantities of paint but avoid slops or drips. Using a good quality opaque paint at this stage will mean one coat is sufficient. Work slowly over each stencil, taking care not to lift the plastic with the movement of the roller.

5 While the paint is still wet, carefully remove each stencil to reveal the base color beneath. It may be helpful to use the blade of a craft knife to lift the stencil corner, thus minimizing the risk of smudging. Clean off the stencils and then repeat the process on the other walls.

Making foil placemats

MATERIALS
- heat-resistant place mats
- sheet aluminum 3mm (1/16 in) thick
- template of design
- foil snips
- contact adhesive
- pins
- protective woodblock
- protective gloves
- hammer
- center punch or nail
- felt

These place mats are a fun project for any time of year. They are remarkably easy to create and bring a touch of practical living to the clean cut, sophisticated environment. Each mat takes only about an hour to make, and uses old heat-resistant bases to protect the dining table. The foil is the kind available in plumbing supply centers, normally in 100 x 100cm (39 x 39in) square sheets. Do take care when you are cutting and folding sharp edges.

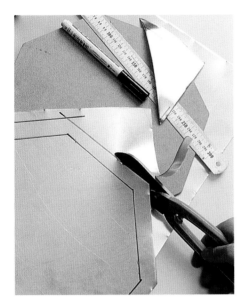

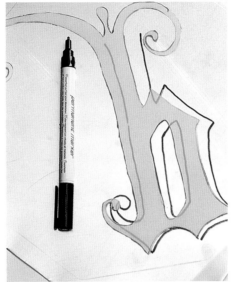

EXPERT TIP

- *These mats were lightly rubbed with abrasive paper after they were made, giving an attractive flat finish and helping to prevent scratches from regular use becoming too visible.*

1 Use a pair of tin snips to cut the metal sheets into manageable sections, somewhat larger than each base mat. Then draw around the mat onto the foil and add a 2cm (1in) border. This border will fold around the edge of the mat and onto the back.

2 Draw the design, back-to-front, on to the reverse side of the foil. If the pattern is to be the same on each mat, use a template so that each design is exactly the same. The image shown here is a copy of one of the stencils used on the walls in the blue room.

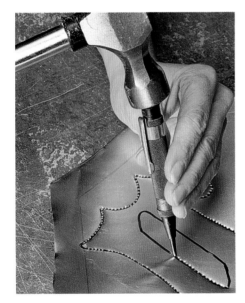

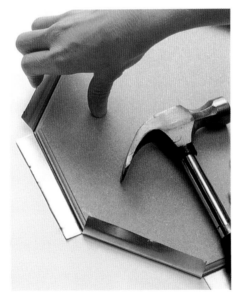

3 Using a nail or carpenter's center punch and hammer, gently tap a row of indented dots along the outline of the marked design. (It's a good idea to first practice on an off-cut of metal in order to gauge how strong the taps need to be.) Remember to use a protective surface, such as a woodblock, beneath the metal.

4 When the design is fully indented into the foil, position the mat upside down on its reverse side. Fold the edges of the metal carefully and tightly around the base mat. Cut a notch of foil away in any angled corners in order to help make a clean fold. It may be a good idea to wear protective gloves at this stage.

5 Use a hammer to gently tack the foil into place around each mat. If necessary, use contact adhesive round the edges as well, to ensure strong adhesion. Any remaining folds of foil can be snipped away and tidied at this point. Then cover the base with a piece of felt to avoid scratching the table surface.

Clean, crisp and simple, white reacts to different lighting, conveying a sense of space, warmth and adaptability.

White & Primary

Nowadays, more and more people are working from home, helping to cut down on the expense, stress and time of travelling to an office every day. However, many people don't have the space or finances to convert a spare room into a full-time working area and places such as the dining room are often used.

Offering a dual purpose space, dining rooms can be used for work during the day and dining in the evening. However, it's important to keep these

PROJECTS FROM
THIS MAKEOVER
SHOW YOU:

• *How to secure wall bolts*

• *How to make a simple*
  flap-up desk

• *How to make a foldaway*
  screen

functions as separate as possible. The practical work area should not be cluttered with distracting tableware from breakfast and, when it comes to a relaxing meal, the presence of papers and other pressure-related work should be kept to a minimum.

This room, decorated in functional white but accessorized with bright primary colors, offers an ideal dual purpose environment. A flap-up desktop provides important daytime working space but is folded for evening use to reveal a decorative detail. A folding screen conceals most of the essential office equipment, such as the computer, files and papers. The practical transformation from office to home space literally takes a couple of minutes and is assisted by the white walls reacting to different light.

CHOOSING PRACTICAL PAINTS

In many cases, the choice of paint finish is dictated by the type and level of room use. For example, velvet or satin alkyd finishes are far easier to clean than flat emulsion, which tend to soak up dirt. However, paints with a sheen finish tend to reflect the glare from sunlight, computer screens and any surrounding colors, which can inhibit concentration. For this reason, a flat finish was chosen for the room – bearing in mind that white is very easy to patch up with a small spare pot of paint. If you are unsure of which paint to use or the extent of the glare, prepare some large boards in both flat and velvet finishes and live with them propped against the walls for a few days before choosing the most suitable type.

SECURING WALL BOLTS

Always ensure that any objects that are fixed to walls are adequately positioned and secured. Shelves and desks must be able to withstand the weight of anything that is to be placed on them, including books, files or even the weight of your arms. Identify the type of wall you have – cavity, drywall or plain brick – before buying the fixings and take time to complete the job properly, in order to avoid accidents and disappointment. To conceal screws completely, try drilling a countersink (using a countersink drill bit) into each screw hole. The small, extra dip provides a comfortable indent in which the head of the screw can sit neatly. Countersink screws are available in most sizes and ensure a good finish to your work.

1 There are various types of wall bolts, including basic plastic plugs (center), special drywall fixings (bottom left) and steel wall bolts, which open like an umbrella as they are screwed in (top left and bottom right).

2 Drill holes at regular intervals in the item that is to be fixed. In the batten for the flap-up desk (pictured on page 112), holes were drilled about 25cm (10in) from each end and then spaced regularly, about every 25cm (10in).

3 Hold the batten up against the wall on which it is to be fixed. Mark the position of the screws by gently tapping a nail through each hole, so that a tiny indent is made on the wall surface. Then drill the holes.

4 Insert plugs into the holes in the wall. Then fix the batten by inserting screws through the wood and into the wall plug. Screw firmly into place, using either a normal screwdriver, or an electric one as shown here.

MATERIALS

- hardboard/white-board
- pencil
- ruler
- saw
- 3 x 5cm (1 x 2in) batten cut to length of desk
- drill and bits
- piano hinges
- screws and screw-driver
- hooks and eyes
- 2 x lengths of chain for side fixings

Making a simple flap-up desk

During the day, adequate workspace is essential. However, when the evening comes around, it's important to try and hide the trappings of working life and relax without the reminders of daily pressures. This simple desk top provides a sturdy, practical work surface during the day and folds away neatly in the evening, conveniently helping to conceal evidence of working life.

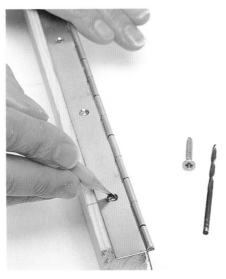

1 Cut a piece of flat wood or white faced board, for the main surface, to the chosen size. Then cut a piece of batten to exactly the same length. It may be helpful to use the length of the piano hinges to determine the length of the desk. For example, to make a 120cm (48in) desk, use two 60cm (24in) piano hinges. This will save cutting metal hinges to the correct size.

2 Fold a piano hinge, the right side out, over the edge of the wall batten. Mark the position of the screws by inserting the tip of a pencil through the holes. Then drill holes through the batten. Once all of the holes in the wooden batten have been drilled, repeat the process for the edge of the desktop, carefully marking and drilling the holes in the same way as before.

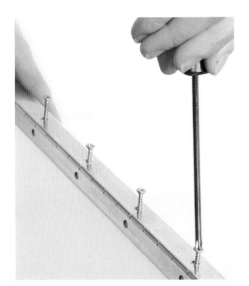

3 Screw the piano hinge to the desktop. Then screw the other side of the hinge to the batten. Make sure that the screwheads lie flush with the hinge, and check that the hinge opens and closes so that the surface will sit flat against the wall.

4 Fix the batten to the wall as shown on page 111. Fix brackets or supporting chains to the edge of the desk top and the wall with the use of hooks and eyes. Saw away any excess chain but keep one end of each chain adjustable, so that the desk can be folded.

MATERIALS

(FOR A 3-FOLD SCREEN)
- 6 pieces of 3 x 3cm (1 x 1in) planed spruce cut to height
- 12 pieces of 3 x 3cm (1 x 1in) planed spruce cut to width
- 50 x ready made dowels
- drill and bits
- wood glue
- woodstain or wax
- 10 meters (33ft) of upholstery webbing
- staple gun and staples
- sheets of paper for each panel (9 were used here)
- varnish
- paper, calico or items to fill gaps in screen

Making a foldaway screen

Computers are a feature in many modern work areas, but they are cumbersome and not particularly attractive. A screen is the easiest method of concealing a computer and much of the paraphernalia that accompanies one. This particular screen took under a day to make and uses dowel joints, which are an effective way of assembling corners without the need for great carpentry skills. The hinges are made of upholstery webbing – an old trick which saves time and complex work. For a larger screen, increase the number of panels.

1 For each panel, cut two tall pieces of wood 3 x 3cm (1 x 1in) to the required height. Then cut four crossways pieces for the horizontal battens. Remember to subtract the thickness of the tall sidepieces. (For example, these were cut 5cm (2in) shorter than the total width of each panel, because the wood is 2.5cm (1in) thick.)

2 Measure and mark out the position of the dowels on the end of each crossways piece. Then mark their corresponding slots on the sides of the tall upright pieces. Drill holes into both the cross pieces and the upright pieces. These holes should be about 2cm (¾ in) deep, or at least large enough to accommodate the dowel.

3 Coat the end of each piece of dowel with wood glue and push them halfway into the holes on the end of the crossways piece. Then push the other ends, again coated in glue, into the corresponding holes on the tall sides of the panel. Press the joints firmly together and leave to dry. If necessary, clamp the pieces together until they dry.

4 Stain or wax the bare wood in your chosen color. Although the wood can be left bare, exposure to temperature changes and general wear and tear may cause the wood to split, so it is always better to provide some kind of stain or varnish protection.

5 Working on the edge of each of the panels, fold the webbing around the wood in opposite directions, creating a pair of s-shaped hinges. Check that there will be room to fold the screen and then staple the fabric into place, at regular intervals on the sides of the panels.

> *EXPERT TIP*
>
> - *Fill the gaps in the panels with stretched calico, parchment or even photographs, using neat pins or staples on the back side where your working will not be visible. To conceal the pins, add lengths of beading with panel pins and wood glue for a final touch.*

MAKEOVER PROJECT

*Warming reds and oranges can be both soft and
vibrant. Use careful lighting to affect the strength of
the tones..*

Red & Orange

The first two colors from the rainbow spectrum, red and orange create a warming environment and are used in this room to convey a spicy, oriental feel. The colors of turmeric, chili powder and paprika, together with burnt shades of red and orange, tone with the dark woods of the floor and table. A mixture of gold and deeply colored accessories complement the reds and catch both natural and evening light. These colors always make a room feel a few degrees warmer than it is,

116

PROJECTS FROM
THIS MAKEOVER
SHOW YOU:

• *How to prepare a floor for staining*

• *How to create a striped wall effect*

• *How to stain a floor pattern*

117

and are ideal for shady, naturally cool areas.

The floor, which features in two of the other rooms in this section, has been further enhanced with a stained, patterned border. Although this can be quite complex to produce, the final effect is stunning and definitely worth the effort.

Remember that red tends to advance and close walls, often making a room feel smaller. To minimize this effect, paint the ceiling pale in a beige flat color. This will help to maintain a sense of height and spaciousness, particularly as the wall stripes tend to draw the eye upwards.

CHECKING THE CONDITION OF A FLOOR

Existing wooden floorboards can be stained and polished to create just as stunning an effect as laying a new wooden floor. The expense involved is considerably less if an existing floor is used, but there are numerous considerations to be taken into account before going ahead. For example, check that the spaces between the boards are no larger than 3mm (less than ¼ in), so that dust and dirt are not likely to get trapped beneath. This will also reduce the presence of draughts.

Check for splits and cracks in the wood. Although boards can easily be replaced, old floors are likely to be made of planks that are different sizes, and additional carpentry expenses may ultimately justify a new floor. However, do not worry about differences in wood tone – sanding should take back the planks to the original raw color. If there are many joins and seams in the floor, remember that the ends of planks tend to absorb more wood stain and so will appear a little darker than the rest of the board. Repair creaky boards by re-fixing the plank with new nails but get rotten wood checked by a professional because damage may have spread beyond isolated boards.

PREPARING A FLOOR FOR SANDING

Spending time on the preparation of a floor prior to staining and varnishing is essential for creating a lasting finish.

A floor that has been carefully sanded and decorated should provide years of service.

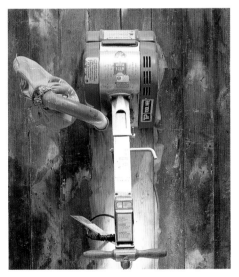

1 Examine the floor thoroughly, inch by inch, and remove all nails, studs or lumps of dried glue. Replace any rotten sections of board, or lift and reposition creaky boards with new nails. Make sure that the nails are fully punched in so they will not tear the sanding belts.

2 Sand the middle of the room with an industrial sander (available from most hire shops). This can be hard work and is easier if shared between two people, unless a special edge sander is used (see step 3). Follow the direction of the boards to avoid scratching the wood.

3 Use a special edge sander for edges and corners (or the whole room if you are alone). Begin the procedure with coarse grade paper, then move on to medium and then fine papers. Wash the newly sanded floor with white spirit or tack rags to remove all traces of dust.

Creating a striped wall effect

MATERIALS
- 5 liters (175½ fl oz) orange acrylic latex velvet
- 2 liters (70fl oz) acrylic scumble glaze
- supermarket carrier bags
- household brush
- masking tape
- pencil and spirit level
- ruler
- 0.5 liter (17½ fl oz) red emulsion

Bold and striking, this striped paint effect is remarkably quick to achieve and demonstrates perfectly how red tends to come forward in a room, advancing ahead of any other color. The red and orange work alongside each other, almost creating a three-dimensional feel to the walls. Bagging, a particularly popular paint effect, works well in these colors to create a soft texture. The orange paint should be slightly shiny so that the red glaze can slide around as the bagging technique is carried out. When dry, the red should remain quite shiny and have textured marks, similar to the appearance of leather.

1 Paint the base orange color on to the walls with at least two coats of acrylic latex velvet emulsion. Very deep colors sometimes need three coats before they intensify to the color on the charts in the DIY stores. Allow each coat of paint to dry for about an hour – or until it is possible to rub a flat palm over the paint and not feel any stickiness.

2 When the top coat is fully dry, mask out the vertical stripes using the method shown in the green and yellow room on page 137. Make a thick acrylic glaze by adding about 0.5 liters (17½ fl oz) of deep red emulsion to 1 liter (35fl oz) of acrylic scumble glaze. Apply the glaze generously to one stripe and then move immediately to step 3.

3 Turn a supermarket carrier bag inside out and crumple it into a ball, about the size of an orange. Dab the wet glaze with the bag repeatedly, working quickly so that the glaze does not dry before the bagging is complete.

4 Peel away the masking tape slowly and carefully as soon as a stripe has been bagged. Do not rip the tape from the wall as it may damage the emulsion paint beneath. Then move on to the next stripe and continue as before.

MATERIALS

- electric sander and sanding sheets
- protective mask
- steel rule
- craft knife
- pencil
- selection of wood stains
- soft artist brushes
- 2.5 liters (88fl oz) floor-quality varnish

Staining a floor pattern

Although it can take time to produce, a stained pattern adds the final touch to any wooden floor. It's a good idea to approach the decoration in stages, helping to break the task into manageable steps and preventing the job from becoming too daunting. The final effect is a room that's both stylish and still a little rustic.

1 Sand the floor in the area of the design. Ensure that all of the varnish and any woodstain is totally removed, otherwise there will be some variation in the shading of the new design.

2 Lightly mark out the design in pencil, using a steel rule. For repeating patterns, use a template. Carefully score each line deeply with a sharp knife, taking care not to let the blade slip.

3 Apply the new stain into each section of the design with a soft brush. The stain will soak into the wood only as far as the scored lines. Any that spreads over the desired lines can be sanded away. Begin with the palest colors and gradually move on to the darker stains.

4 Varnish the whole area completely with at least four coats of good quality floor varnish. Make sure that each coat is fully dry before applying the next layer, and gently rub down the surface with fine grade abrasive paper between coats for a really smooth finish.

Earthy tones can add a touch of style to most rooms. They provide a welcoming warmth and sense of comfort.

Stone & Copper

Soft and warm, yet also extremely stylish, natural colors such as stone and copper are popular choices for many people. The natural, earthy feel of these textures make them ideal for a homely environment, yet the sharp lines and touch of chic also take the room just beyond the boundaries of conventional decorating. This particular room is inspired by autumnal shades and the rough texture of milled stone, as well as by an impulse to be somewhat experimental and non-

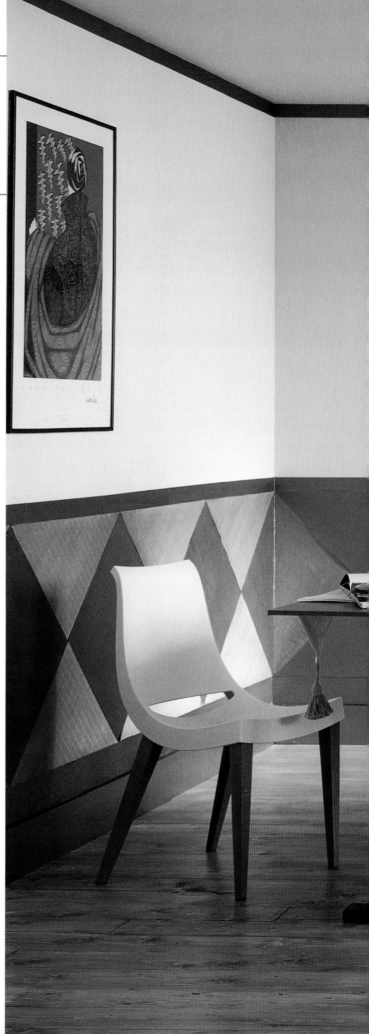

124

PROJECTS FROM
THIS MAKEOVER
SHOW YOU:

• *How to texture walls*

• *How to stipple table legs*

• *How to make a stone*
  encrusted vase

125

conformist. The area below dado height is painted in the same copper paint as the border at the top, but the effect appears somewhat different. This is because the paint has been coated over corrugated card, which is then applied to the wall at opposing angles so that the light catches the paint in different ways. The directions of the card ripples create a combination of velvet and suede effects. Corrugated card is soft and tends to squash and damage fairly easily, so avoid using it in busy areas such as family dining rooms or play areas. However, remember that sections of card can always be replaced easily if they do become damaged.

CHOOSING TEXTURED PAINT

Paint does not always have to be perfectly smooth and flat. Indeed, sometimes a textured finish can be an attractive solution to difficult, rough surfaces or small cracks. Exterior masonry paints are the toughest and most durable paints available, and give excellent coverage. Lightly textured paints, such as the cream used here, are non-reflective and have a gritty feel. For more texture, add clean, coarse sand to paint or try painting over textures such as dried leaves or sisal cord which have been glued to the wall with waterproof adhesives or a glue gun. However, in choosing to use a textured paint, bear in mind that future redecorating may be made more difficult – particularly if you wish to return to a smooth finish.

TEXTURING WALLS

Unusual color and texture were the controlling factors in choosing the tones for this dining room. In addition to juxtapositioned sheets of corrugated card, the cream walls are coated in a rough, textured exterior paint made with granules of sand and marble. This flat effect contrasts beautifully with the velvet and suede effect of the lower wall. The result is a warm, stylish room that reacts to different degrees of light exposure throughout the course of the day.

1 Paint the walls above dado level with one or two coats of textured masonry paint, preferably mixed with sand or marble dust. The area below the dado level should be left unpainted to ensure adhesion of the card.

2 Carefully cut out square sheets of card (corrugated on one side, plain on the other) to go around the room. Then cut out twice as many half squares. Finally, cut out strips for borders at the top, bottom and dado.

3 Paint the rippled surface of each card with one good coat of copper colored paint. It may be easier to use a gloss roller for this task, although take care that paint is adequately spread throughout each ripple.

4 Fix the card sections to the wall using a hot glue gun or glue designed for attaching plaster moldings to walls. Do not use wallpaper paste because it separates the card and will cause the textured face to fall away.

Stippling trestle legs

MATERIALS
- 500ml (17½ fl oz) brown or ginger
- satin paint
- 250ml (8¾ fl oz) alkyd-based scumble glaze
- 1 tube raw umber artists' oil paint
- small bottle of paint driers
- stippling brush
- small household brush

The table for this particular room was made from a simple piece of hardboard wood cut to size and some pine trestle legs. It can be dismantled and folded (using the same style of piano hinges as shown on page 112) for ease of storage, or made in one piece as a permanent item of furniture. Whichever option you choose, make sure that the fixtures are adequately secure and that the table can bear the weight of table decorations and crockery. The table top is painted with two coats of copper paint and the legs have been given a delicious chocolate stipple. This textured finish is easy to achieve and helps to add some color to the room and create a sense of contrast.

E X P E R T   T I P S

• *Pure, quality stippling should not be cloudy but appear as an uninterrupted, smooth expanse of tiny dots. However, some people do prefer the cloudy variation because it is much faster and easier to achieve.*

• *Small or intricate spaces can be difficult to stipple because the hand needs to be constantly moving backwards and forwards as each stroke is applied. In these cases, such as the inside of the trestle legs, either leave the wood unglazed or apply the glaze but do not stipple the surface.*

• *For additional protection, varnish the table legs 2–3 days after stippling.*

1 Coat all of the bare wood in a light brown or ginger colored satin paint. This alkyd-based paint takes a while to dry but provides an important base for the stippling effect. If necessary, apply a second coat to ensure the finish has a slight sheen. Leave the wood to dry, following the guidelines on the paint tin.

2 Add a squirt of raw umber artists' oil paint to about 250ml (8¾ fl oz) of alkyd-based scumble glaze. If necessary, add a teaspoon of driers, which will help cut down the drying time of the glaze from about three days to one. Stir the mixture thoroughly, until the glaze has a smooth consistency similar to that of jam.

3 Apply the thick glaze to the painted surface with a brush, covering sections about 0.5m (2ft approx) at a time. then move immediately on to step 4. This ensures that the glaze does not have time to dry before the stippling action takes place. Applying glaze to any larger area could present difficulties later.

4 Stipple the surface of the glaze by jabbing a stippling brush or thick household brush quickly and repeatedly on to the surface. Aim for about three jabs per second, so that small pinprick marks are left in the thick glaze. Return to step 3 and repeat. Leave the legs to dry fully before fixing them to the table top.

MATERIALS
• terracotta vase or urn
• wire brush
• 1 liter (35fl oz) molding adhesive
• spatula or scraper
• 1 x bag small stone chips

Making a stone encrusted vase

Adding a touch of further texture, this ordinary terracotta pot makes a tasteful transition from the exterior to the interior. By coating the outer surface in a crust of stones, the pot becomes an attractive decorative feature and adds to the rustic, earthy feel of the room. The effect is remarkably quick and easy to achieve, taking about only an hour to complete, before leaving the pot to dry overnight.

EXPERT TIP

- *Gravel and stone chips are readily available from garden centers in a variety of natural and artificial colors. Small pebbles can also be used for this technique but need applying one by one, like the pieces in a mosaic. If the thick layer of adhesive begins to dry before the stones have been applied, remove it with a scraper and reapply some fresh adhesive. Do not add new adhesive to old as this will create an uneven surface.*

1 Although raw terracotta will not need preparation, rub down any pots that have shiny surfaces with a stiff wire brush. This will help to roughen the exterior so that the molding adhesive can grip firmly.

2 Using a spatula or scraper, apply a thick layer of decorative molding adhesive or tile glue all around the pot. Work in relatively small sections so that the glue does not begin to dry, before moving on to step 3.

3 Press handfuls of stone chips or gravel onto the wet adhesive. Be generous with the stones and press them firmly in to the adhesive.

4 Patch up any bare places by pushing individual pieces of gravel into the adhesive. Then stand the pot aside to dry for several hours or overnight.

131

Cheerful and lively, greens and yellows create a relaxed, happy environment with a slightly rural, country-style feel.

Green & Yellow

Bright and vibrant, greens and yellows tend to conjure images of nature and summer, bringing a welcoming sense of fresh air to any dining area. Indeed, green is commonly associated with hunger and appetite, and is a popular choice of decoration for many restaurants. However, the shade of the green should never be too bright – strong greens tend to reflect off surfaces, making skin, in particular, appear rather unhealthy and sallow. The greens used here include sap green and oxide of chromium.

PROJECTS FROM
THIS MAKEOVER
SHOW YOU:

• *How to stain a wooden*

floor

• *How to create a checkered*

paint effect

• *How to make a shelf tidy*

In family homes, dining areas tend also to be used for painting and drawing activities. Yet children's toys and play utensils can create unwanted clutter when the room is to be used for a relaxing meal. In this room, the shelves have been given hanging covers, providing useful concealment for stored items and creating a decorative feature. The floor is made of tongue and groove spruce and has been stained in a dark oak, water-based stain. Several coats of varnish mean that it can be cleaned with a mop and is resistant to normal wear and tear.

MAINTAINING HYGIENE

Any dining area should be kept clean and to a high level of hygiene, but this is even more important if the space is also used as an active family room. Toys, games and drawing activities all generate dust and grime. Cracks and bumps in a wall surface provide an ideal harbor for dirt and germs, as well as affecting the quality of the final paint finish. For this reason, it's important to make sure that any room where hygiene is a major consideration must be smooth and to a degree washable, able to withstand wiping with gentle cleaning fluids. However, ammonia-based cleaners can act like paint strippers on some surfaces, particularly those coated in alkyd-based paints. Wherever possible, use water-based paints with a glaze and carefully fill cracks before applying the first coat. Velvet sheen paint, which is used to create the cheerful checks here, has the added bonus of being easy to clean and maintain. However, never scrub this type of surface as any abrasive action may cause the paint to lift.

STAINING A WOODEN FLOOR

Whether made from newly laid or revitalized floor boards, wooden floors need good preparation if they are to withstand average daily use. Basic cleaning and sanding of an old floor is featured below but, once this task is complete, the process of staining and varnishing is the same for both new and old floors. See page 122 for advice on patterns.

1 Wearing socks or stockings, to avoid additional dirt, sweep the floor. Then wipe the entire surface with white spirit, remembering to work from the furthest corner towards the door, to avoid getting trapped. Leave the surface to dry for a few minutes, with the windows open, to maximize ventilation.

2 Again working from the far corner, apply stain with a household brush, cloth or foam brush. Although overlapping while the stain is still very wet will not cause any visible marks, avoid brushing wet stain over any areas that are already dry. Try to work quickly, completing one board at a time

3 Leave the boards to dry, following the manufacturer's guidelines on the tin (this type of stain normally takes about an hour). Then wipe the floor with a dry cloth to remove any excess stain that has not soaked in fully. Apply a second coat as before and leave to dry for several hours.

4 Apply a good, floor-quality wood varnish with a large household brush. Work along the grain and leave the varnish to dry fully before walking on the floor. The greater the number of coats of varnish, the more hard-wearing the surface. Most experts recommend a minimum of four coats.

Creating a checkered painted effect

MATERIALS
- acrylic latex velvet base paint
- pencil
- spirit level and measure
- masking tape
- 1 liter (35fl oz) acrylic scumble glaze
- artists' acrylic paints for staining glaze
- household brushes
- long piece of spare
- wood (optional)
- emulsion glaze coat

Once a basic technique of colorwashing has been mastered, more intricate designs such as checkered or striped patterns are easy to achieve. Here, the transparency of the glaze work allows the base color to glow through, providing depth and intensity of color where the stripes cross over each other. Painting these effects does not take long, although it's important to spend some time measuring and masking the wall, to ensure a good finish.

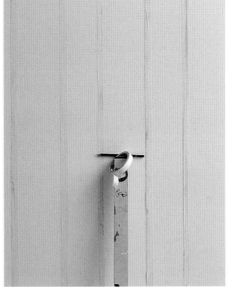

1 Paint the walls of the room in the yellow base color, using a paint that has a slight sheen, such as acrylic latex velvet. For the best results, choose a base color that is paler than the desired color of the stripes or checks. If you are painting on to a dark base, more than one coat may be required.

2 When the base coat is fully dry, mask out the vertical stripes with the aid of a spirit level or plumb line. Remember to position the masking tape on the outside edges of the darker stripes, so that the areas to be painted are not obstructed. The stripes shown here are 25cm (10in) wide.

3 Mix a glaze, using the acrylic scumble glaze and about a tablespoon of artists' acrylic paint or colored emulsion paint. However, do not add too much color – the aim is to maintain the transparent qualities of the glaze.

4 Apply the glaze in a thin coat to the masked out stripes, using a household brush in a random, crisscross motion. Only overlap wet areas – wet glaze meeting dry glaze will cause undesirable lines and marks.

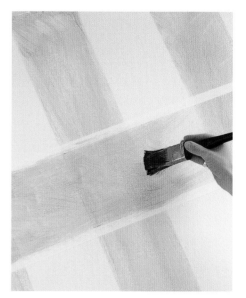

5 When the vertical stripes are dry, remove the tape and then mark and mask the horizontals. To save measuring, this can be achieved by marking a long piece of wood with correctly spaced lines. Then work along the wall and use these marks as guidelines for marking the horizontal stripes.

6 Most homes do not have perfectly straight ceilings so check the horizontals carefully with a spirit level. If the ceiling is not quite straight, make tiny adjustments of about 1cm (½in) at a time on each horizontal. These alterations will be less obvious than one top or bottom stripe that is definitely out of kilter.

7 Mask off the horizontals in the same way as the verticals, checking that the lines are always at right-angles. Then apply glaze to the horizontal areas, again using a criss-cross motion. Remember to avoid leaving a stripe half-coated, otherwise the glaze will begin to dry before more wash can be added.

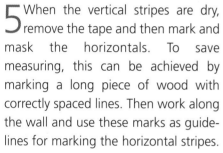

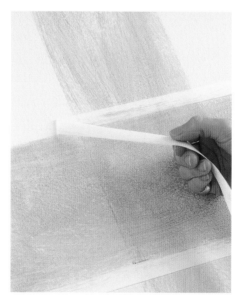

EXPERT TIP

- *Horizontal stripes can only be adjusted if the ceiling is no more than 5cm (2in) out of line. If the ceiling is distorted any more than this, horizontal stripes (no matter how greatly they are adapted) will actually emphasize the problem. A ceiling that is severely uneven dictates that the walls should have only vertical stripes, rather than the checkered effect used here.*

8 Carefully remove the masking tape while the glaze is still wet. Peel the tape slowly back on itself, making sure that the tape does not pull the paint base away from the wall. Low-tack or cheap masking tape is ideal because it is less sticky than expensive brands.

9 For extra longevity, give the walls a single coat of emulsion glaze coat, in either a velvet or flat finish. Although this appears cloudy and milk-like when it is wet, the glaze dries clear to provide an additional protective coat to the walls' decorative finish.

Making a shelf tidy

MATERIALS
- ready-made steel or wooden frames
- masking tape
- marker pen
- center punch & hammer
- drill and bit
- hooks and eyes
- pliers

A solution for common storage problems, these picture frames conveniently conceal children's paints and drawing materials. The frames are joined in such a way that they can be easily moved, and offer an amusing alternative to curtains, blinds or cupboard doors. Furthermore, the simplicity of the joins means that the frames can be easily moved around. This encourages proper use of the shelves, rather than other storage 'solutions' that are awkward and difficult.

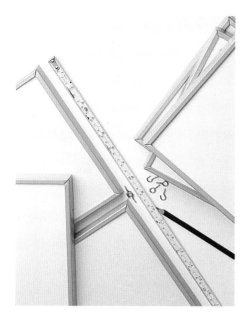

1 Establish the length of the hang needed to cover the shelves, including the gap that the hooks and eyes will use. It can be useful to have a specific frame design in mind but make sure that you have enough matching frames to cover the relevant area.

2 Join the frames carefully with masking tape, in order to establish the position of the holes on each edge. The top frame of each column should have holes marked on both the top and bottom so that it can be fixed to a hanging hook on the top shelf.

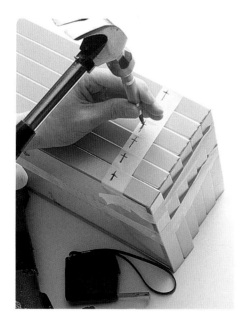

3 Begin each hole by tapping a center punch in place. This will prevent the drill bit from slipping as the hole is drilled. Then carefully drill the holes to the required depth, taking care to use a drill bit that is the correct size for the hooks and eyes, to ensure a tight fit.

4 Insert hooks and eyes into the drilled holes, and hooks into the top shelf, from which to hang the cascades of frames. This step can be quite fiddly, particularly as hooks and eyes are difficult to handle and a tight fit is important. A pair of pliers may be useful for the final turns.

KITCHEN
MAKEOVERS

Buying a new kitchen is without doubt an enjoyable and exciting venture. It can, however, be expensive and there are other, cheaper ways to transform the kitchen you already have. Paint is inexpensive and offers you an immediate way to update not only your walls but your floors, furniture and accessories too. Today's demand for color has led to a huge growth in the range of paint colors available. There are literally hundreds of colors to choose from in a number of finishes suitable for various surfaces.

This section should be used as a practical guide to selecting paints and colors for your kitchen. Discussion on color theory will help you to choose and use color in the home. Practical advice on paint products and their suitability is combined with inspirational examples showing the use of color and its effect. The selection of projects undertaken here can all be adapted to suit your own ideas, for your own kitchen.

In this section, the same kitchen has been given six makeovers using a range of different color schemes and styles. Although the kitchen has remained the same, the floor and the splashback have been changed to different materials, and the door knobs have been changed each time. The color schemes vary from a bright and sunny Caribbean theme, to the warm and earthy colors of Morocco. These countries inspired certain color tones and combinations, but there are many others to choose from. The colors of the neutral kitchen create a soft and restful atmo-

sphere, whereas the 1950s color scheme is more lively and exciting. If you possess stainless steel appliances and cooking utensils you may be inspired by the lime green kitchen, or try your own choice of color with the same paint effects. Blue is a color that is often associated with country kitchens—the blue kitchen featured in this section has been distressed with crackling paint effects. I hope you can see how very different one kitchen can appear in a different color, using a different paint effect.

All the paint effects and techniques shown throughout this section can be used in many different colors and styles. Experiment first and try out your ideas on cardboard, lining paper or on off-cuts of wood. Keep your test boards in the kitchen for a few days, see how they change throughout the day in the different light levels and take your time deciding if you like them there —or not!

In these makeovers color is not only employed in paint but also in other elements, such as fabric in the curtain making project, or tiles on the mosaic table. The individual projects allow as much or as little of that particular look to be re-created. With in-depth information on preparation and basic techniques, an absolute beginner to home decoration can have the confidence to put these ideas into practice. Everything you need to know to get started is contained within these projects.

The kitchen is the heart of the home, so do not overlook the importance of creating a happy and joyful environment. Painted kitchens can be re-painted again and again over the years as your choice of colors changes. There is no excuse for putting up with a decor you don't enjoy! There are many elements to consider when decorating your kitchen but there are no right or wrong colors to use. There is a great delight to be had in painting and enjoying colors—we need color like we need light. So take responsibility for your kitchen now and make it a room to enjoy!

Using color in your kitchen

Every kitchen, like every person, has its own unique character. When choosing clothes for a person, there are many different aspects to consider—the size, the shape, the natural coloring and the personality. To make the best choice for your kitchen, consider carefully all the different aspects involved.

KITCHEN LIGHTING

The first consideration may be that of lighting; good natural daylight can be quite a luxury in many city flats and houses. If you are more dependent on artificial lighting, remember that many colors, especially yellows, change considerably in this type of light. Some light bulbs cast a blue hue, giving yellow a cooler, greeny appearance. Other warmer-colored bulbs project a yellower golden light. If you are going to change the lighting in your kitchen, make sure you do so before finally deciding on a particular color for your decorating scheme. You could end up with something completely different from what you had planned!

While you are actually painting your kitchen, switch the lights on and off occasionally to check the effect and always try to paint in natural daylight when you can. It is helpful to test your color first on an odd scrap of wood or hardboard, then leave it in the room for a few days. Look at it at different times of the day and notice if and how it changes. It is also helpful to leave a sample of the wall color next to it. See how these colors

Two of these kitchens illustrate using opposite colors (top left and bottom right). Orange and blue are opposite colors and so contrast and complement one another dramatically. In contrast, the colors in the kitchen bottom left are all from the same area of the color wheel and therefore blend more quietly. Blue and white is a traditional color combination.

147

sit together and decide, over a few days, whether you grow to like this combination. Try to paint as large a sample board as you can. Better still, try to paint large areas of the color on the wall. If this is in water-based paint, it can of course be painted over again quickly and easily.

COLORS ON A COLOR CHART

When choosing colors from the little color cards you buy in shops it can be suddenly daunting to see the same color in all its glory on a whole wall. The full impact can prove too strong. The lighting in paint shops is often quite different from the lighting in your home. Take the paint charts out of the shop, and look at them on the street in natural daylight.

Try to test a color in as large an area as possible. Although not available at many paint shops, some outlets do supply small tester pots of flat water-based paint—an inexpensive and practical way of testing colors—especially those that might look very similar on a color chart but clearly different on a wall.

If it is not possible to paint samples directly on to your wall, paint on to lining paper. Cut pieces of this to size and hold them up to the wall. Sometimes four walls painted in exactly the same color can look quite different throughout the day, and quite different from each other.

FUNCTIONAL CONSIDERATIONS

Nowadays, many people use the kitchen as a dining room too. If

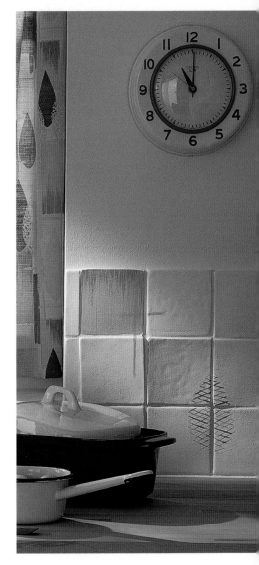

the two functions of your kitchen are in one and the same area, you could paint different elements such as the table and chairs to match or complement the units. In the blue kitchen, for example, the table and chairs were painted in the darkest cream color used on the walls. Then a simple painted flower pattern was added using the same blue as used for the kitchen. This is a very easy method of bringing together different elements.

If the kitchen and dining area are separate, you could connect them through color. You could, for example, carry the kitchen wall color through to the dining area and treat it in a different way. If it is a colorwash, you could gently alter the tone, making it softer and warmer as you approach the dining area. Or, you could keep the same color but add a painted frieze or border as you leave the kitchen area. Choose something from the same theme, such as the squares from the neutral kitchen, or the pattern from the Moroccan kitchen.

SIZE AND SPACE

Light and cool colors project a feeling of space. Cool colors, such as soft blues and greens, recede:

the walls appear further away and the space appears larger. The opposite effect is achieved with warmer colors, such as yellow, red and orange. The walls appear to advance towards you and the space seems smaller. Darker colors make a room look smaller, while lighter colors create space and light.

Consider the size of your kitchen in terms of the impact of your chosen colors. The 1950s kitchen, for example, may be too lively and the colors too strong in a very small area. The neutral kitchen would bring a feeling of space and light into a small area. The Moroccan kitchen would make a small space look smaller but at the same time more cosy and intimate. Think about the effects you would like to achieve in your given space. If you have a small kitchen, don't automatically try to make it look bigger. Warm and intimate colors might be much more suitable.

KITCHEN LAYOUT

Consider the existing layout of your kitchen. Do you want to bring a disjointed layout together with the colors you use or do you want to separate certain areas through color? In the lime green kitchen, for example, different tones of lime green were used on the walls. The back wall was a deeper shade of lime green, and the two adjacent walls were a lighter shade. Using different strengths of a particular wall color has the effect of bringing certain walls forward and taking others back. In a long thin room, for example, you might want to use darker tones on the walls furthest away to bring them into the

room, and lighter tones on the walls closest together so they appear further apart.

When painting blocks of color, as in the 1950s kitchen, you might want to use this effect to link in and balance different elements of your kitchen. In this makeover, a separate cupboard was painted in the same style to make this part of the central kitchen. You could do the same with doors, windows, tables, chairs or other pieces of furniture.

Color can also add weight to certain items. Dark warm colors can add weight to a surface, giving a more solid and fixed appearance. The opposite effect is achieved with light cool colors. The colorwashing technique in the Caribbean kitchen (see page 188), for example, could be graduated to extend to the height of a wall. If the wash is darker on the lower areas of the wall and you gradually lighten the color the higher up you paint, it will have the effect of lifting the wall, raising the height of the ceiling and the length of the wall.

CONCEALING UGLY FEATURES

Most kitchens have their fair share of elements you wish you could hide. These may include pipes and radiators and boxed-in taps. Try to paint as many of these as possible to lose them into the wall, skirting board or door. Do remember, though, to use the correct type of paint on different surfaces. A paint finish on hot pipes will flake off in no time, so do use an appropriate solvent-based paint to blend these into the wall or the units.

SOOTHING
Blue

There is an enormous range in the color blue. It is a primary color and sits between green and red on the color wheel. Green blues, such as aqua and turquoise, tend to be cooler than the redder blues, such as lavender. The blue stool is painted with a middle blue with no green or red added, just black and white to create different tints and shades.

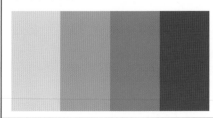

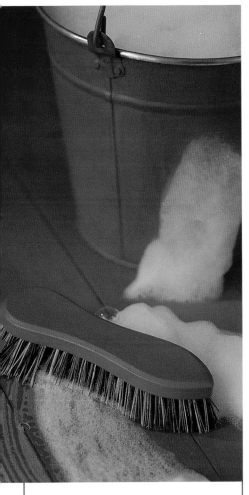

Any pipes, taps or boxes on the wall or skirting board can also be painted. Treat radiators in the same way. If they are to be painted the same color as the wall (the best way to lose them if you have no radiator cover or box) remember not to use water-based paint as it will crack or flake off. Use a solvent-based paint to match as best you can. Try to avoid using solvent-based glazes or varnish on radiators. As the radiators heat up, the linseed oil in glaze and alkyd-based varnish will discolor and cause the radiator to stand out yet again! This is especially evident in blue glazes that turn noticeably green. Any radiator boxes and shelves will also be affected by the heat and suffer in the same way.

HIGHLIGHTING ATTRACTIVE FEATURES

There may be some elements of your kitchen that you choose to make a feature of through your use of color. You may have a cornice or a ceiling rose, for example. These could be brought out by washing color over them using the same method as color-washing with scumble glaze (see page 191). There were no cornices to deal with in these six kitchens, but you need not have a fancy cornice to treat this way—a simple curved cornice can be lightly washed and gently brought into the walls.

Do not neglect the skirting boards either. In all of the six kitchen treatments in the section, the skirting board was brought into the kitchen by treating it in the same way as the doors.

BRILLIANT
Red

Red appears the strongest, most aggressive color of the primaries. It excites and enlivens and it is thought to induce conversation, so the type of red should be well chosen! On the color wheel, red sits between violet and orange. On the violet side red becomes deep crimson, heavy and majestic, while on the orange side red becomes fierce and fiery.

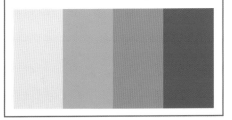

LINKING COLORS

The two major existing features to consider in any kitchen are the worktop and the floor. Where possible, do try to connect these colors in some way to the colors you choose for your kitchen scheme. For example, a white worktop could be balanced with a white sink, white appliances, and a white base coat showing through a colorwashed wall. Mottled and wooden worktops are easiest to deal with as they offer many different shades to pick out and use in the walls, or the unit doors. This is, of course, not always necessary—it just makes for a gentler, softer connection.

Wooden floors, like wooden worktops, are easier to pick colors from as there are often many different colors in the wood itself, especially in pale wood. Wooden floors can easily be painted—in the 1950s kitchen the floor was painted gray to match the skirting and frame of the kitchen. There are many products available to make floor painting as easy as possible; acrylic floor paint, linoleum paint and tile paint are now available and easy to use.

Window blinds and curtain fabric are also very important influences for color. The 1950s kitchen was painted entirely around the curtain fabric. When you are planning your decorating scheme, try to take into account all the different elements in your kitchen before painting, as it is easier to adapt the paint color to work with what you have than the other way around.

SUMMERY
Violet

Violet is a secondary color formed by mixing red and blue, and can range from pinky-lilac to lavender. It can be a warm and gentle color, but in its darker and redder forms it may appear a little heavy. Used in its purest and softest forms, however, it can both soothe and uplift, as evident in beautiful summer flowers.

CITRUS
Yellow

Yellow is a vibrant primary color, placed between green and orange on the color wheel. In its green form yellow becomes limey and acid, fresh and sharp. In its orange form it becomes warm and golden. Yellow is the color closest to sunlight and in its purest form creates a special glow —like gold—joyous and lively.

CEILING COLOR

Most kitchen ceilings are white. It is clean, fresh and bright and usually works well in most kitchens. Kitchens are, after all, working areas and a white ceiling allows the light to reflect clearly on to the work surfaces, making it much brighter and easier to work. Even the fairly dark Moroccan kitchen retained a white ceiling for this reason.

Off-white, creamy colors may work better for your particular color scheme, though, and will not affect the light too much; they could in fact add a little more warmth and intimacy to the room. A darker warmer color on the ceiling will advance towards you so the ceiling appears to be lower than it is. A lighter cooler-colored ceiling will have the opposite effect, so the ceiling will appear higher.

USING PATTERN

Pattern can enhance and echo various shapes in a room. In the neutral kitchen a very simple pattern along the side edge of a wall was used. The square shape was taken directly from the size, shape and coloring of the splash-back ceramic tile.

Inspiration for patterns can be sought in many ways. Try looking at pattern source books, old tiles or pictures and postcards of patterns. The pattern used in the Moroccan kitchen was taken from a floor tile.

You can use paint and color to soften patterns. If you find your pattern looks too strong, rub it down lightly with sandpaper. You could age the pattern further by

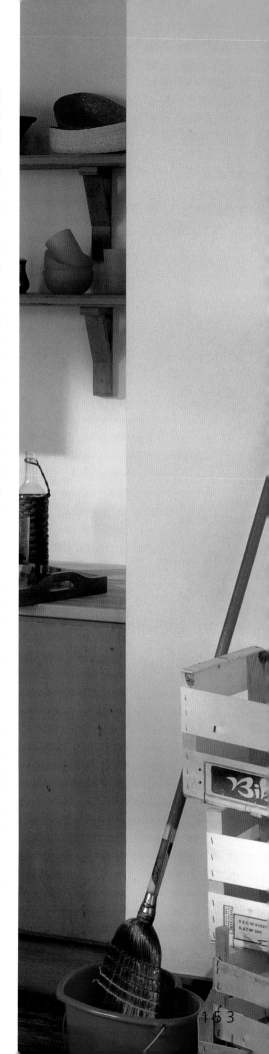

using a brown wash (see the Caribbean kitchen doors, page 192). This will soften the overall effect of a pattern. Pattern on a mottled background has a gentler effect, and the contrast is already softened. The patterns in both the neutral and the Moroccan kitchens were painted on to a mottled base.

Pattern is usually used quite sparingly in kitchens. They are busy spaces with different heights and shapes to contend with. Worktops and cupboards become full with patterned cups and crockery, food packets, and so on, all of which have contrasting colors. So pattern in the kitchen should be used carefully.

PSYCHOLOGICAL IMPACT OF COLOR

The most important consideration in choosing color for your kitchen is the effect it has on you and your mood. There are basic loose guidelines about the psycholog-

REFRESHING
Green

Green is the color formed by mixing blue and yellow. In its yellow form it can take on a striking character that is a dazzlingly fresh and cool lime green. In its blue form, sea green, it can be a cool, soft and yet vibrant color. Green is often mixed to an earthy tone to simulate the colors of foliage. It is the color most associated with nature, and so promotes a healthy, restful feeling of comfort.

WARMING
Orange

Orange is made from yellow and red. It is a powerful and splendid color, the color of log fires and sunsets. In its yellow form orange is light and lively; in its redder version it becomes richer, more fierce and flame like. Orange in decoration is often toned down with paler colors to form apricot tones, or mixed with browns to form burnt ochres and warm rustic terracottas. It is a warming color, rich and majestic.

ical impact of color. Certain colors excite and enliven (for example, red and orange), some uplift (like golden yellow) while others calm and relax (such as blue).

Green is said to be a soothing color, evoking the natural surroundings, and is a good color for a kitchen that leads out to the garden. This is an example but also a generalization, as one color can receive many different responses. Everyone has their own personal associations with specific colors and reactions are subjective. Primarily you need to choose colors you enjoy. Consider also whether you want a kitchen to relax in, like the neutral kitchen or the blue kitchen, or whether you want one to promote alertness, activity and creativity, like the vibrant 1950s kitchen, or if you prefer the warm, cosy feeling of the Moroccan-style kitchen. The only rule is to enjoy the effects you create.

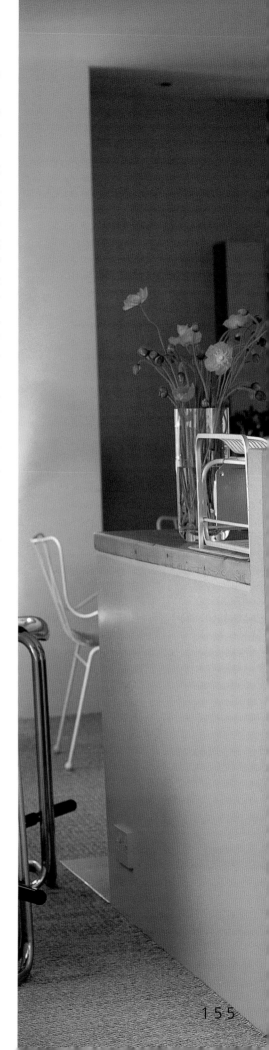

MAKEOVER PROJECT

A cornflower-blue scheme looks stylish yet relaxing.
Pale walls and bare wooden floors prevent the blue
being too overpowering.

Tuscan Blue

This strong rich blue is taken from an old country kitchen in Provence or Tuscany. The color is of cornflowers and deep blue glass. As the blue is slightly violet in tone, it has the effect of warming the room wonderfully, while the pale walls prevent the effect from becoming overpowering.

The blue paint has been chipped and cracked, showing patches of a brownish-gray base to give the effect of age. For a stronger antiqued effect you could use a lighter base color. Alternatively,

PROJECTS FROM
THIS MAKEOVER
SHOW YOU:

- *How to create a chipped paint effect*
- *How to antique with crackle glaze*
- *How to decorate a chair*

you could use strong colors together such as turquoise and deep blue, or bright green and deep blue. Experiment first with little tester pots of paint—you might be surprised at the colors you end up choosing!

The walls in this kitchen were painted in an off-white color, then washed with an older dirtier white. In this way, the central areas are kept lighter while the corners, edges and sides are darkened, giving a softer antiqued look rather than an even colorwash. It also softens the newness of a flat painted wall.

The table and chairs were painted in the darker wall color and the chairs were given a simple hand-painted flower motif in the same blue as used on the cupboard doors. Leftover paint can be used on all sorts of things!

The door knobs on the units are small wooden knobs which have been given the same paint effect as the doors. Try to buy untreated wooden knobs to paint as they will not need to be prepared.

This cracked antiqued look is particularly good for cupboards needing repair, as any lumps and bumps in the doors just add to the effect—as will any further knocks and chips. This look also disguises any repairs you make with spackling compound; you won't have to worry about sanding to create smooth surfaces. However, remember that once you use crackle glaze on your doors it is very difficult to paint over.

CREATING A CHIPPED PAINT EFFECT

This decorating technique is very effective in achieving a mellow look of age and wear through time, an effect that has become very popular and an interesting way to break up solid color. The chipped paint effect can be used in conjunction with crackle glaze (see page 160), as can be seen in this Tuscan blue kitchen.

1 Apply a base coat on the surface and leave to dry. Using a thin paintbrush, carefully apply small lumps of beeswax to the surface. The areas to concentrate on most are the edges and corners as these are the most likely places to receive the brunt of any wear and tear.

2 Allow the beeswax to dry overnight and then apply the water-based top coat. If you will not be using crackle glaze (see page 160), two coats of water-based paint will be required.

3 Allow the paint to dry, then carefully chip off the lumps of beeswax using a filling knife. This will reveal small patches of the base coat, giving the effect of age. Apply a coat of acrylic clear varnish over the surface to seal it.

EXPERT TIPS

- *A chipped paint effect can also be used in conjunction with color-ageing to enhance further the antiqued look of a piece.*

- *For a flatter, softer worn effect, rub a candle or a wax stick along the surface, concentrating on the door edges. Unlike the beeswax the candle can be painted over immediately—the paint will not stick to the waxed area and can be rubbed off quite easily.*

MATERIALS
• household paintbrush
• crackle glaze
• flat water-based
  paint: dark and pale
  blue
• cotton cloth
• acrylic clear flat
  varnish

Antiquing with crackle glaze

Using crackle glaze on a surface has the effect of making the paintwork crack, giving it a worn and aged look. The effect can be used on its own or together with the chipped paint effect, as seen on the blue kitchen units. To use both together, apply the crackle glaze straight onto the beeswax before applying the paint. This project illustrates how to use crackle glaze on its own.

1 Using a household paintbrush, apply crackle glaze over the surface in an up-and-down motion. Keep all of the brushstrokes even and regular as this will help determine the direction of the cracks. Allow to dry.

2 Once the crackle glaze is dry, apply a coat of dark blue flat water-based paint, keeping the brushstrokes even and straight in an up-and-down direction. Don't stop the brushstroke halfway down the surface as this could show up later in the cracks.

3 Leave the paint to dry and wait for the cracks to appear. To speed up the drying time, you can dry the paint gently with a hairdryer, moving the hairdryer all over the surface.

4 When the cracks appear, dab a clean cotton cloth into diluted pale blue water-based paint and rub this into the surface; this will highlight the cracks and break up the color. When dry, apply two coats of acrylic flat varnish to seal.

EXPERT TIPS

- *Experiment to see how the cracks will appear by testing a small area first. You could apply either one or two coats of crackle glaze (two for larger cracks), but always follow the instructions for your individual product as they do vary from one product to another.*

- *Once you have used crackle glaze on a surface it is difficult to re-paint it as the glaze will keep on working and cracks will keep on appearing. To overcome this, sand down the surface to remove the crackle glaze. Alternatively, cover the surface with a fine spackling compound, then seal this with shellac to prevent the glaze coming through any more. This is a laborious process and best avoided!*

Decorating a chair

MATERIALS

- medium-grade sand-paper
- wooden chair
- cream water-based paint
- household brush
- tape measure
- pencil
- blue water-based paint
- or artist's acrylic paint
- fine artist's brush
- fine-grade sandpaper
- cloth
- raw umber artist's acrylic paint
- acrylic clear varnish

Painting old furniture is a good way to disguise unsightly cracks and holes; these can be repaired and then covered with paint, never to be seen again. Before painting a chair with water-based paint, you need to rub it down to remove any dirt, varnish, wax or previous paint layers, then apply a coat of primer. Alternatively, you could use an alkyd-based paint, such as satin enamel;

in this case, you then need to use alkyd-based paint for the painted pattern. It is important not to mix oil and acrylic materials. This chair was painted with water-based paint on top of a coat of white primer. The design—a simple pattern of dots—was applied by hand, varnished, and finally colored and aged with a small amount of artist's acrylic raw umber.

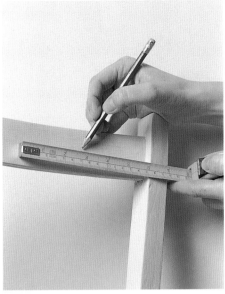

1 Having prepared and primed the chair, apply a coat of cream water-based paint using a household brush. Allow to dry, then apply a second coat so that the chair is covered evenly. Leave the chair to dry.

2 Measure the backrest of the chair, then mark out regular positions for the dotted pattern with a pencil. The blue to be used for the pattern is dark enough to cover the pencil mark but if using lighter colors it is best to use a paler marker such as chalk.

3 Mix up a small amount of blue paint for the design, using either water-based or artist's acrylic paint. Using a fine artist's brush, carefully paint in the floral dots, following the pencil marks. Leave to dry, then rub the painted pattern lightly with fine-grade sandpaper.

4 Use a tack cloth to wipe away any dust left by the sandpaper. Mix a little raw umber artist's acrylic paint with acrylic clear varnish, then brush this over the chair to create an aged look. If the brown looks too heavy, wipe it off quickly before it dries, and try again.

MAKEOVER PROJECT

Subtle natural shades create a gentle and relaxing decorating scheme, allowing you to accessorize with bright splashes of color.

Neutral Shades

Pale creamy colors are the most popular for painted kitchens. These subtle natural shades form a gentle, relaxing and undemanding background that will enable you to bring color into the room in other ways.

Look at natural objects for inspiration when choosing soft neutral colors for your kitchen scheme. Pebbles and seashells can be found in beautiful subtle shades in every color. Look closely at such everyday food as garlic cloves, rice, bread and cheese for pale neutral shades.

PROJECTS FROM
THIS MAKEOVER
SHOW YOU

• *How to blend and mix*

colors

• *How to paint a wall*

pattern

• *How to stain a floor*

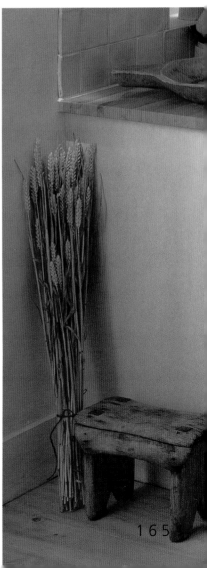

165

The crackled tiles in the kitchen were the starting point for this color scheme. The tiles contained pink and gray tones with dark gray cracks. The pink was echoed on the walls with a very light colorwash. To do this, a pale pink was washed on to the walls first and then softened with a semi transparent white wash and very small amounts of gray here and there. This was warmed up in places with touches of gardenia (the color of clotted cream). For colorwashing in gentle colors, it is best to buy shades that are darker than you actually require and then lighten them with white paint. Once the paint is diluted and added to scumble glaze it appears much lighter, so if you use subtle shades to begin with they are likely to be lost in the finished effect.

The painted wall pattern was used to echo the shape and colors of the tiles along the wall. This pattern was made up on the spot but you could design your own pattern in any number of ways. You could, for example, make a border of straight lines or turn the squares on their edge to make a pattern of diamonds.

Gardenia was also used as the base color for the unit doors. It helped to bring together the cream tones in the beech worktop and the pale pine wood floor. Soft gray was applied over the creamy, gardenia base in downward streaks; this was then followed by white (see below). The door knobs were painted in the same way; the darker gray tones remaining in the recesses accentuate their shape. This same process could also be used for paneled doors.

BLENDING COLORS

This method of blending colors on a surface is easy to do, but it is best to experiment first on a piece of card-board or lining paper until you achieve an effect you are happy with.

1 Spoon some gray water-based paint and some acrylic scumble glaze into a paint tray without mixing them together. Dip a household paintbrush first into the paint and then the glaze, and then paint this in downward strokes on to the surface to be decorated. Keep the color light and even.

2 Allow the paint and glaze coat to dry. Then dip your brush lightly into white water-based paint so that only a tiny amount of paint is on the bristles, and brush this roughly over the top, allowing streaks of the gray to show through. Continue to paint over the surface until the colors are blended to your liking.

MATERIALS
• ruler
• pencil
• wall tile
• flat fitch or artist's brush
• water-based paint

Painting a wall pattern

This simple wall pattern is painted using water-based paint onto a water-based colorwash. A colorwashed wall gives a gentle background for such hand-painted patterns or stencils. To create this shape you can draw around a wall tile. To paint more intricate shapes and patterns, you may find it easier to cut a stencil or use transfer paper to transfer a design.

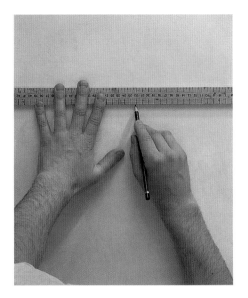

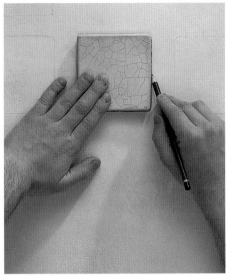

1 Measure the wall and decide where you would like the pattern shapes to go. Mark the positions lightly on the wall with a pencil. These marks will be used as positional guides when drawing the design on the wall.

2 Following the positional guides, draw lightly around the wall tile with a pencil to build up the wall pattern. This can extend over a whole wall or just a small area. A random pattern can look effective, but if you prefer you can make a strong geometric design with precise angles. Do not worry about the pencil marks; they will be covered with paint at the next stage.

EXPERT TIPS

- *To make the pattern appear less solid, add some acrylic scumble glaze to the water-based paint. Put a small amount of scumble glaze and a separate small amount of water-based paint in the paint tray and dip into both with your brush. Use the paint tray like a palette and test the consistency first. Build the color up slowly. It is always easier to make the color stronger—but more difficult to remove the paint to achieve a lighter shade. If you find the squares too dark, you will have to paint them white and start again.*

- *For an even softer effect, you could go over this pattern with a light colorwash. You will have to colorwash the whole wall for an even shading.*

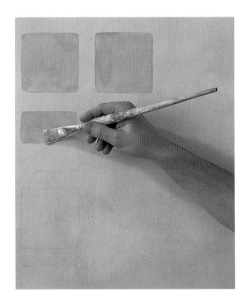

3 Using a flat fitch or artist's brush, paint in the penciled shapes with water-based paint, without going over the edges. For an even softer effect, you could go over this pattern with a light colorwash. You will have to colorwash the whole wall for an even shade.

Staining a floor

MATERIALS
- floorboards
- protective face mask
- floor sander
- edger
- knotting solution
- cloth or brush
- artist's acrylic paints
- water
- bucket
- household brush
- cloth
- acrylic flat or satin
  floor varnish

This project shows how to create a natural-looking stained effect on pine floorboards. Many proprietary wood-stains can look rather heavy and unnatural, and yet untouched pine can look rather flat and new—not as mellow as the effect achieved here. The way to create this effect is an unconventional treatment but one that works easily, and, once varnished, is as durable as any other floor finish.

A wash of thinned artist's acrylic paint is applied to the wood and gently rubbed with a cloth to achieve a shading that looks natural and mellow. Two or three artist's acrylic paints can be mixed to achieve the precise color required. The resulting colors are generally of good quality, usually a purer more intense color than that achieved with a water-based colorwash.

1 Check your floorboards for loose nails. Then, wearing a protective face mask, sand the floorboards with a floor sander. Floor sanders can be hired; always follow given instructions. Most sanders have a dust bag but still produce a large quantity of fine dust. Start by using coarse-grade sandpaper, if necessary, and gradually work your way down to fine-grade sandpaper.

2 Use an edger to reach right into the corners and edges of the floor. These can be hired with floor sanders. As with a floor sander, always work from a coarse-grade to a fine-grade sandpaper to produce a smooth finish.

3 Seal any knots in new wood to prevent them from bleeding resin. Apply knotting solution over any knots using a cloth or brush. For pale wood floorboards, such as pine, use white knotting solution, which dries transparent. Apply the solution only to the knot. As the solution seals the knot and wood, the stain will not soak in as effectively as it will on untreated areas.

EXPERT TIPS

- *Before staining floorboards, make sure that the floor is dust free. Wipe the floor with a tack cloth to remove tiny specks of dust.*

- *If the grain of the wood rises when you apply a water stain, allow it to dry thoroughly then lightly sand it off to a smoother finish.*

4 Squirt a small amount of artist's acrylic paints from their tubes into a bucket and slowly dilute them by adding water a little at a time. Stir the mix constantly. Test the stain first on a piece of wood. Apply the wash over the floorboards in sweeping brushstrokes in the direction of the grain. Rub off areas that may appear too heavy with a cloth.

5 Allow the stain to dry completely, then apply two or three coats of acrylic flat or satin floor varnish over the surface. Do not use alkyd-based varnish as this will yellow and ruin the subtlety of the staining effect.

MAKEOVER PROJECT

The spicy colors of Morocco — warm terracottas and vivid blue-greens — create a mellow atmosphere of coziness and relaxation.

Moroccan Spice

The colors featured in this warm, mellow kitchen —rich, earthy terracottas and vivid blue-greens— evoke the colors of Morocco, and the warm spicy tones of chili powder, nutmeg and turmeric.

Exotic Morocco was the inspiration for this kitchen. Naturally colorwashed walls, earthy terracotta-colored pots, exotic tiles and ceramics and vivid blue-green patterning all work together to create a warm and lively atmosphere.

The cupboard doors are warm orangey browns

PROJECTS FROM
THIS MAKEOVER
SHOW YOU:

• *How to paint a door*

• *How to transfer a pattern*

• *How to make a mosaic*
tabletop

with some grayer tones in the patterning. These grayer, more muddy, colors were taken from the colors in the floor. The deep chili red was added to the door pattern and to a simple pattern of dots along the edge of the shelf. Although these warm colors seem to advance towards you and therefore have the effect of making the room look smaller, they also seem to increase the temperature of the room, making for a warm and cosy kitchen.

The units were painted with a sand-colored base and then washed in a light spicy red, which produced a slightly mottled base color. A Moroccan pattern was then painted over this using transfer paper. This particular pattern was adapted from a Moroccan tile design of which there are hundreds to be found in design source books; you could also look through travel books and holiday photographs or kitchen accessories for design ideas and inspiration.

The walls were washed a few times in light sandy colors on a base of white water-based paint.

The wash was built up with three layers of color, one slightly yellow, one more muddy and the other more orangey brown. The window frames and surround were painted in a muddier color found in the painted pattern on the doors. The dark wooden floor and the wooden worktop fitted in well with these earthy tones.

PAINTING A DOOR

This basic technique is very simple but one that many people do not know. Applying paint correctly gives you a good, even coverage of paint and it may mean only having to apply one coat instead of two. The mistake a lot of people make is trying to apply paint in an up-and-down motion—it is much more difficult to achieve an even application in this way. To paint an average-sized kitchen door, a 6.5 cm (2½ in) household brush is particularly suitable.

> *E X P E R T   T I P*
>
> - *If you have paneled doors, a different method of painting applies. First paint the center frame beading and the panels. Then paint the outer edge—the two horizontal top and bottom bars first, then the two vertical sides. Apply paint vertically for the panels and the vertical sides (stiles) and then horizontally for the cross bars (rails).*

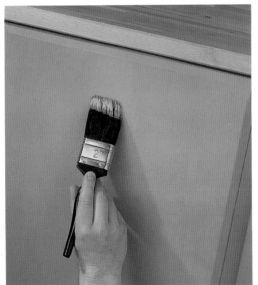

1 Starting in the center of a door and working quickly, apply the paint liberally in every direction, up, down, side to side and diagonally, to cover the whole surface completely.

2 Then, without pausing, brush the wet paint down, up and down again over the entire surface to smooth and even out the application. Work at speed so that the paint remains moveable; if you leave the paint to dry slightly before smoothing the brush-strokes, the result will look uneven and streaky.

Transferring a pattern

MATERIALS

- tape measure
- plain or graph paper
- pencil
- low-tack masking tape
- transfer paper
- fine artist's brush
- acrylic paint

This method is a simple way of transferring a pattern, and for an intricate pattern such as this one, it is easier to use this transfer method than to cut and use a stencil. Transfer paper can be bought in different colors—blue is the most common, but on a darker base yellow or white would stand out better.

The transfer paper is water based so once the pattern has been painted on, any remaining marks can be wiped off very easily with a damp cloth.

First draw the pattern onto graph paper—you can always use a photocopier to enlarge and reduce your design to fit particular doors.

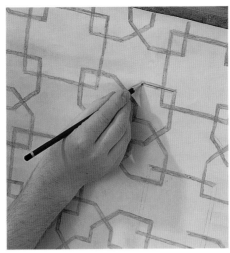

EXPERT TIPS

EXPERT TIPS

• *Draw the different elements of a design on tracing paper before transferring them on to the main sheet. In this way, an even scale can be retained. Mark the actual door size onto the page and draw the design to fit as neatly as possible.*

• *An alternative method is to use photocopies of your design. These could be enlarged and reduced to scale, then stuck together with sticky tape.*

• *It is also helpful to draw a rough color sketch before you start, as certain patterns work best with certain color combinations.*

• *Once the pattern is complete and if you feel it looks a little strong, lightly rub it back with fine-grade sandpaper or add a colored varnish (like that used in the painted chair project, page 162).*

1 Measure the cupboard doors with a tape measure. Then cut a piece of paper the same size as the doors and draw out your pattern on the paper in pencil. You could copy a pattern from a tile design like this one, from a design source book, or you could even design your own pattern.

2 Using low-tack tape, stick a sheet of transfer paper on to the cupboard, chalky side down. Then tape the penciled design on top of this. Using a pencil, trace over the design outlines to transfer the pattern onto the door. When you have finished, lift up one corner of the transfer paper to check that all of the design has transferred. If necessary, go over any faint lines again. Then remove the paper.

3 Using a fine artist's brush and acrylic paint, carefully paint over the transferred lines. You could vary the color throughout the pattern just by dipping the brush occasionally into another very similar color. Don't worry if your painted line wobbles slightly as you paint—this adds to the hand-painted charm of your design.

Making a mosaic table

MATERIALS
• table
• glass tiles
• tile nippers
• protective eye
  goggles
• tape measure
• pencil, optional
• PVA glue
• ready-mixed grout
• flexible spatula
• cloth

This simple mosaic design was created using small glass tiles—the kind often used at the bottom of swimming pools. The tiles can be bought loose, but are usually supplied on a paper backing, which is easily removed after being soaked in water. The tiles in this design were cut and applied to a wooden tabletop that had been scratched and damaged beyond repair. Mosaic tiles can be applied to most surfaces—even an old plastic tabletop can be transformed with mosaic tiles. They provide a hard-wearing surface that is also practical for garden furniture outdoors. The tiles are available in a vast range of colors and the design can be as complicated as you like. This table features a simple circular design but you could create a more detailed pattern and cut the tiles to fit.

EXPERT TIPS

- *To create a more subtle effect, use small ceramic tiles in place of glass tiles. These are supplied in uneven shapes and have a rich natural coloring to them. They are more expensive than the glass tiles but for small areas and intricate patterns the effect can be stunning.*

- *Another, cheaper alternative would be to use broken crockery. Break old plates and saucers gently with a hammer to produce random shapes that can be used to build up a colorful and interesting mosaic pattern.*

1 Cut a few tiles with tile nippers to experiment with different pattern formations. Wear protective eye goggles when using tile nippers to protect against flying fragments of tile. Angle the nippers over one half of the tile rather than all the way across when cutting it. This will achieve a more precise cut and prevent the tile from shattering.

2 Arrange the tiles in the desired pattern, experimenting with whole and cut shapes to see what works best. This design uses both whole tiles around the edge and cut tiles in the center. Measure the tabletop and ensure that the design will fit. For a complicated design, you can draw the design out on the tabletop and cut the tiles to fit.

3 Using a strong PVA glue or panel adhesive, stick the tiles down in place on the tabletop, leaving small gaps in between. Tile adhesive can be used for quicker applications, but sticking tiles individually allows you to work more slowly. Run your fingers over the glued tiles to ensure they are secure.

4 Apply ready-mixed grout over the glued tiles using a flexible spatula. Cover the entire surface, then wipe off excess grout with a damp cloth. Grout will remain in the spaces between the tiles. Allow the grout to dry, then clean the tiles with a damp cloth.

MAKEOVER PROJECT

*Lime green teamed with chrome produces a smart,
practical and vibrant decorating scheme, ideal for
keeping you alert and busy.*

Lime Green

This contemporary kitchen makeover, decorated in varying shades of lime green and accented with stainless steel kitchen accessories, looks clean, fresh, practical and very vibrant. Limes are an obvious inspiration for this color scheme; inspiration is also found in young spring flowers and plants.

Green is a color associated with freshness and health, and is therefore highly appropriate for a kitchen.

PROJECTS FROM
THIS MAKEOVER
SHOW YOU:

• *How to paint a cupboard*

• *How to fit metal gauze to*
a cupboard

• *How to paint a window*
frame

Stainless steel is a practical kitchen material, functional and clean, and it teams up well with lime green.

The unit doors were painted a deep strong lime green and then colorwashed and blended with a lighter shade to break up the color, and create a gentler mottled effect. In keeping with the stainless steel accessories, new modern steel handles were fixed to the doors.

Steel sheets were then bought cut to size and glued to the wall to make a stylish splashback. This was sealed for protection.

The two glass doors on the kitchen cupboard were replaced by metal gauze. This can be bought at builders' merchants and cut to size with a pair of scissors. It is easy to fix the gauze to the doors (see page 184) and it completely changes their character. There are many different types of metal gauze suitable for this project. The main requirement is that it is stiff and strong and does not bend too easily. An alternative to metal gauze is perforated zinc, which was traditionally used to cover food before the days of refrigerators. The inside of the cupboard was painted deep violet. Used in small quantities, this vivid color seems to break up the lime green well. It is always effective to paint inside cupboards with bright and lively colors but do make sure that the paint will adhere.

The walls were painted white, then washed in pale lime green; a darker shade was used for the back wall. Using the leftover paint, a few wooden storage boxes were painted in the two different lime greens, white and violet.

PAINTING A CUPBOARD

Painting a kitchen cupboard is straightforward if you pay attention to the little details. Careful masking is essential to avoid smearing an adjoining edge with paint, and using the right paintbrush can help you produce a professional and neat finish.

1 Before you begin painting, use masking tape to section off the worktop. Masking tape can be bought in varying widths. If the paint soaks into the wood it will be difficult to remove. Then, using a household brush, paint the cupboard door.

2 Once the front of the cupboard door has been painted, open the door and paint the top edge of the cupboard if this is visible when the door is closed. Use a small fitch brush to paint into the corners and edges of the cupboard; a household brush might not cover the small surface evenly.

EXPERT TIPS

- *If you drip or smear water-based paint on a surface, dab it with a cloth dipped in methylated spirits (if it is too late for soapy water); use mineral spirits to remove solvent-based paint.*

- *Many modern kitchen doors clip on and off. It is easier to paint the doors actually in position and use a tiny brush to paint around the inside hinge. For touching up inside edges, take the doors off and the drawers out and then paint along the inside edge.*

MATERIALS
• ruler
• metal gauze or wire mesh
• scissors
• tack pins
• hammer

Fitting a metal gauze door

This project is not as difficult as it seems—taking the glass out of the cupboard is probably the hardest part—and it completely changes the character of the cupboard. When choosing metal mesh to use, make sure it is coated and will not rust. You can usually take home samples of mesh to think about before finally choosing a design.

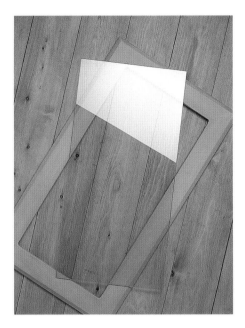

1 Take the cupboard door off its hinges and carefully remove the glass panel by loosening or removing the clips holding it in position. Work slowly and methodically all around the panel to avoid breaking the glass.

2 Turn the cupboard door face down. Measuring from the rebate of the door, calculate the size of metal gauze required; it will probably be the same size as the glass.

3 Using a pair of household scissors, cut the metal gauze to the required size to fit the door. Check that it fits in the rebate at the back of the door.

4 Carefully lay the piece of metal gauze in the rebate of the door. Secure it in place with tack pins, hammering them in gently at 5 cm (2 in) intervals all around the rebate. These will not be visible from the front. Rehang the door on the cupboard to finish.

MATERIALS
• all-purpose spackling
  compound
• filling knife
• sandpaper
• dusting brush
• primer or undercoat
• household brush
• water-based paint
• lining fitch
• window scraper,
  optional

Painting a window frame

There are ways of making window frame painting an easier task; the right tools and equipment can help tremendously. This window frame has been painted in lime green, the same color as the kitchen units; too often woodwork is left white and not brought into the kitchen. As with most aspects of deco-rating, preparation is very important and the first steps of filling holes, rubbing down and undercoating are vital for achieving a good quality top coat. The same methods employed here can also be used on other woodwork, such as door and window architraves and skirting boards.

1 Fill any holes in the window frame using all-purpose spackling compound. Rub the surface well with sandpaper to achieve a smooth finish, then use a dusting brush or a dry soft brush to prepare a clean dust-free surface.

2 If your window frame is new wood, apply a coat of primer. If the frame is old and heavily repaired, apply undercoat. Many undercoat primers are now available as one product. Apply the primer or undercoat as smoothly as possible as this will affect the quality of the top coat. Leave to dry, then sand lightly and dust it as before.

3 Apply the top coat of water-based paint, using a lining fitch (a brush that has an angled head) to aid the cutting in of paint around the glass and where the frame meets the wall. Using a good quality brush will improve the finish.

4 When dry, use a window scraper to remove any paint that has splashed onto the glass. The smooth blade of a window scraper will scratch off paint without scratching or damaging the glass in any way.

Combine the sunny Caribbean colors of hot pink, bright yellow and turquoise to create an exciting and lively kitchen scheme.

Sunny Caribbean

This vibrant-colored kitchen with its bright turquoise, sunshine yellow and hot pink decor uses colors of the Caribbean to create a lively happy environment.

For inspiration in choosing bright and cheerful colors for your kitchen, look at exotic flowers, bright fabrics and patterns, food products and packages from the West Indies.

In recent years, these colors have become more popular for use in interior decoration. Most paint

PROJECTS FROM
THIS MAKEOVER
SHOW YOU:

• *How to colorwash a surface*

• *How to age a painted
surface*

• *How to crackle glaze and
paint terracotta pots*

189

companies now stock a range of suitable paint colors of this kind.

Although strong and exceptionally vibrant, these colors are enjoyed in a Caribbean climate under the bright West Indian sunlight. In the northern United States, however, especially in certain houses, they may appear too harsh and strong. This is where ageing techniques can be used to good effect. The colors can be broken and softened considerably with antique washes and other ageing and broken color effects.

On the kitchen doors, a bright turquoise was applied to a brown base that shows through in places where the paint has been chipped off. This effect was achieved by applying lumps of beeswax over the surface; once dry, turquoise water-based paint was used over the top and the beeswax scraped off with a filling knife to reveal patches of the brown base color beneath (see page 159). This paint effect also creates the impression of age and wear. A wash of burnt umber was applied over the turquoise to age and soften the color. The wooden door knobs were painted to match. The walls were colorwashed in a sunshine yellow water-based paint on top of a white base. The shutters, chairs and table legs were painted in the same way as the doors with bright pink water-based paint on top of a dark brown base coat.

The dark brown base color used on the doors and shutters is evident in the floor. This dark floor contrasts with the vibrant colors used in the kitchen and holds the decorating scheme together.

COLORWASHING A SURFACE

Colorwashing is a technique for achieving a mottled broken color effect on a surface. For this project water-based paint and acrylic scumble glaze were used. The wash was applied over a base coat of white water-based paint. The surface should be well covered and even with no visible cracks, as imperfections will tend to show up more once the wash is applied. To create a more subtle, gentler effect, go over the walls with a second wash once the first is dry.

EXPERT TIPS

- *An alternative way of colorwashing is to brush on the glaze as before, then wipe it off and rub it in with a soft cloth rather than a brush in certain areas. This creates a patchier, rougher-looking finish.*

- *You can use acrylic colorizers instead of water-based paint for a more transparent look. A more controlled application would be achieved on a less porous surface, such as low sheen or acrylic satin.*

1 Prepare the glaze by mixing water-based paint with acrylic scumble glaze, adding more paint as desired. Brush the prepared glaze over the surface in all directions, tapering off at the edges.

2 Without leaving the glaze to dry, soften the glaze with a dusting brush. Brush over the glaze to soften the brushmarks and create a hazy cloudy finish.

Ageing a painted surface

MATERIALS
- acrylic clear varnish
- burnt umber artist's acrylic paint
- household brush
- dusting brush

In this project, a bright turquoise cupboard door is toned down and softened considerably by a simple ageing technique using artist's acrylic paint. This technique allows bright colors to be used in a decorating scheme without them dominating the room.

1 Place a spoonful of acrylic clear varnish on a piece of wood or old plate, then squirt a blob of burnt umber artist's acrylic paint next to it. Using a household brush, dab the tips of the bristles first in the varnish, then in the paint, touching only the tiniest spot of paint first—you can always add more to it.

2 Brush this mixture onto the surface of the door in an uneven way, spreading the color wherever you want it to be. For an aged appearance that looks authentic, apply more color where dirt and grime would usually collect, such as around the edges of the door or around the door knob.

3 Before the varnish and paint mixture has dried, go over any brushmarks that are visible on the surface with a dusting brush. This will produce a softer, more blended finish.

Glazing terracotta pots

MATERIALS

- terracotta pot
- blue water-based paint
- household brush
- crackle glaze
- yellow water-based paint
- artist's brush
- dead flat acrylic varnish

As terracotta is an absorbent porous surface, water-based paint can be painted straight onto it. The bold colors used throughout the kitchen have been used again to jazz up these terracotta pots. The crackle glazed effect is an easy and fun way to use strong colors together—the red under the pink and the blue under the bright yellow, for example. It also creates an impression of age. The same effect was used on the units of the blue kitchen (see page 156). As water-based paint dries quickly, it can always be re-painted in a different color if you are not happy with the final look. Once the pots are varnished, they will be wipeable and hardwearing.

1 Apply a base coat of water-based paint in your chosen base color. Allow to dry and apply a second coat. The cracks will appear in the direction you apply the paint.

2 Once the base coat is dry, apply the crackle glaze in the same direction as the base coat. For strong cracks, as shown here, allow the first coat of glaze to dry out completely, then apply a second coat.

3 Once the crackle glaze has completely dried, apply the top coat of water-based paint in a contrasting color in the same direction as before. Apply the paint in one sweeping motion and do not go over an area that has just been painted—this will pull the glaze off and ruin the effect. If this does happen, let it dry, then start again. Use enough paint just to cover the area. Allow to dry, when large cracks will appear.

4 Line the rim of the pot once the inside and outside are dry: apply a new base coat, then a coat of glaze, and then the top coat. Use a small artist's brush to create an even finish. Leave the pot to dry completely, then apply two coats of dead flat acrylic varnish over the pot to make it water-proof and wipeable.

BEDROOM MAKEOVERS

The bedroom is often the last room in the home to be decorated. And yet it is the one room where you can really express yourself. In this section, the same bedroom has been given six makeovers using a variety of color schemes and painting styles to show you how different one room can look. Paint is inexpensive and offers an immediate way to update not only your walls but your floors, furniture and accessories too. Today's demand for color has led to a huge growth in the range of paint colors available.

Color is a wonderful tool; it can literally transform everything it touches, and it is a vital part of our lives. It affects us in a way that we cannot fully appreciate: it can induce a range of feelings within us, and can cause us to respond in ways that we do not understand. Color can assist in making changes to our moods from happy to sad and from good to bad. Our unique ability to define differences in color separates and distinguishes us from all other species. With so many magazines dedicated to homes and interiors, paint manufacturers are producing more and more color ranges, giving us more color choices than ever before.

This section should be used as a practical guide to selecting paints and colors for your bedroom. Discussion on color theory will help you to choose and use color in the home. Practical advice on paint products and their suitability for different surfaces is combined with inspirational examples showing the use of color and its effect. The selection of projects under-

taken here can all be adapted to suit your own particular ideas for your own bedroom.

The color schemes used in this section vary from fresh, bright lemon and lime to warm terracotta, and from moody blue to a riot of color in the Matisse-style bedroom. In addition to flat painting of walls and woodwork, several paint effects are introduced. If you have been discouraged in the past from attempting paint effects because of the complicated process involved with alkyd paint, acrylic paints will be a welcome discovery. They can be adapted very easily and are available from most hardware stores. Acrylic varnish was also used to create several of the room makeovers. The process of mixing small quantities of water-based paint with acrylic varnish is very easy and it allows you to experiment with different forms of application.

All the paint effects and techniques shown throughout this section can be used in many different colors and styles. Experiment first and try out your ideas on lining paper or off-cuts of wood. Keep these

in your bedroom for a few days and see how they change throughout the day in the different light levels.

In these makeovers color is not only enjoyed in paint but also in other elements such as fabric and wallpaper. The individual projects allow as much or as little of that particular look to be re-created. With information on preparation and basic techniques, an absolute beginner to home decoration can have the confidence to put these ideas into practice. Everything you need to know to get started is contained within these projects.

Use these color schemes and project ideas to give your bedroom a new lease of life; after all, there is no excuse for putting up with decor you don't like. And an advantage of experimenting with paint and color is that if you don't like the finished result, you can re-paint the surface and start again.

The tremendous sense of achievement one experiences when looking at the end result is very pleasurable.

Using color in your bedroom

Color is one of the most wonderful and versatile tools of interior decoration. With the use of paint you can transform the darkest room into a light, bright space, or the loudest decor into a muted paradise of sophistication. Knowing how to mix and use color is crucial to the success of any interior. However, because color is essentially an abstract concept, many people find it difficult and bewildering to fathom. This lack of confidence is largely due to an ignorance of the basic principles of color. In color theory, as with most things, there are certain rules and guidelines that should be followed. As your confidence grows, you can even try to break a few.

THE COLOR WHEEL
The color wheel offers one of the most important ways to understand color. It is a simplified version of the spectrum: circular in shape, it is an arrangement of the primary colors of red, yellow and blue, and the secondary colors of orange, green and violet. From these colors, all other colors are made, including grays, browns and neutrals.

Color can be used to change the shape and size of a room. Rich strong colors like crimson diminish the space and create a warm, dramatic environment. Cool blue creates an airy quality which can also be accentuated with accessories in contrasting colors. Soft pastel colors blend together for a calming environment. Color can also be applied to a divided space for interest.

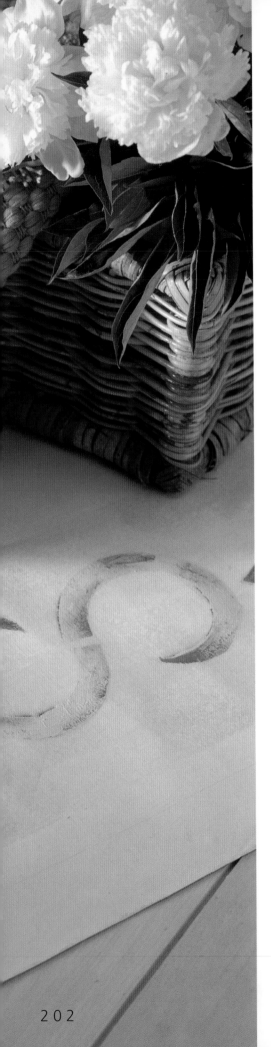

Primary colors are equidistant on the color wheel. A primary color cannot be made by mixing any other colors. These primary colors can be mixed together in varying proportions to produce every other color in the spectrum. When two primary colors are mixed together in equal quantities they produce a secondary color. For example, when blue and yellow are mixed they create green; when yellow and red are mixed they create orange; when red and blue are mixed they produce violet.

A tertiary color is made by mixing an equal amount of a primary color with the secondary color next to it on the color wheel. By adjusting the proportions of the primary or secondary colors you can create a wide range of subtle colors.

There are two basic ways in which colors react with one another: they will either harmonize or contrast. This is easy to see on the color wheel: colors that harmonize are close to each other while those that contrast are placed far apart. If you want to use colors that harmonize, choose a section of the color wheel and work with just those colors that are adjacent to one another; for example, blue with blue/green or blue with blue/violet.

The colors situated opposite one another on the color wheel are known as complementary colors. There are three main sets of complementary colors: red and green, blue and orange, and yellow and violet. When two colors of the same tone and intensity are used in a room,

they will intensify each other, causing the eye to jump rapidly from one color to the other, thus giving a shimmering effect. When opposite colors meet they create impact. They enhance each other and produce a vibrant visual sensation; each color will appear brighter against its neighbor than it would alone. For example, green and red can work well together in a room when used in the right proportions; equal amounts of each color can result in a jarring shimmering effect, but small hints of red in a predominantly green room can be very exciting. It is sometimes better to use near or split complementaries, such as turquoise and pink. In this room, highlights of red, green, purple and orange were used in the accessories to emulate the busy vitality of a Matisse painting.

The use of one warm color alongside a cool one helps to create a feeling of balance within a room. Colors are either warm or cool. The warm colors are those that fall within the yellow-orange-red sections of the color wheel, while the cool colors range through the purple-blue-green segments.

COLOR AND MOOD

One of the most important aspects of color is that it is emotive; it stimulates all the senses, not just the eyes. Color can be used to suggest and to accentuate the mood of a room, as well as create an emotional response from the viewer. It can trigger a flow of images, emotions and sounds. Blue, for example, makes us think of sky and sea, mountains and streams. Depending on the color and tone used, it can denote freshness and lightness or melancholy and alienation. Yellow is the color that conjures up images of sun and flowers but it can also be harsh and acidic. It is therefore vital that the correct color and tone is chosen.

TONALITY

When choosing a color, it is important to consider the depth

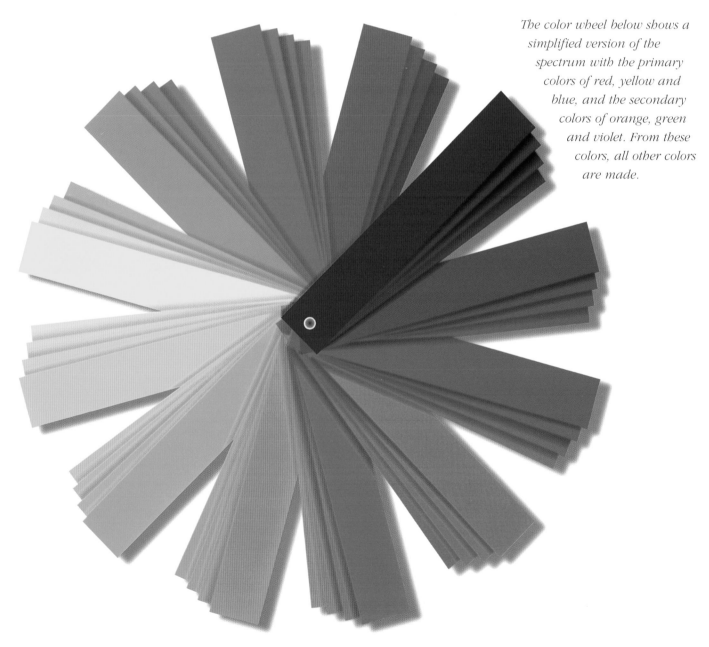

The color wheel below shows a simplified version of the spectrum with the primary colors of red, yellow and blue, and the secondary colors of orange, green and violet. From these colors, all other colors are made.

of tone you desire. The tonal value of any color will change with the effect of light. The more a surface faces away from the source of light the darker it will become. The framework of light and dark areas that make up a room is often what initially attracts attention and will give an immediate introduction to the mood or atmosphere of a room. Tones and colors are modified by adjoining colors; a color that appears dark when next to a white wall may well seem to have a lighter tone when surrounded by other colors. Colors and tones should never be regarded in isolation, but in terms of how they relate to others around them. All colors and tones are influenced by neighboring ones. When two colors are viewed side by side, the contrast between them is enhanced. Each touch of color added to the room alters the relationship of the colors that are already there.

COLOR HARMONY

Harmony is possibly the most subtle and evocative of all reactions between colors and can be used with great effect to create mood in a room. While contrast is dramatic and may emphasize a special feature or area of the room, harmony is gentle and easy on the eye. There is harmony between those hues that lie on the same section of the spectrum or color wheel, for example between the yellow and green featured in the lemon and lime room (see page 220). This is a combination frequently found in nature in the harmony of a spring landscape. Although harmonious schemes are often the most

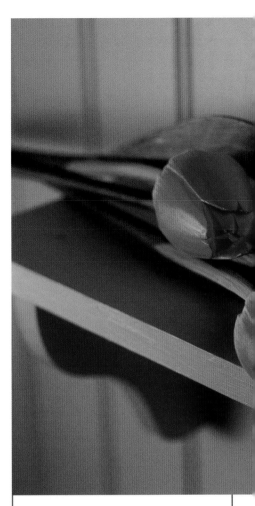

(see page 220)

BRIGHT
Pink

Pink is an extraordinary color. It can range from pale cotton candy, through sugar-almond pink to subtle salmon. Pink works well with turquoise, its complementary color and with the colors on either side of it on the color wheel, violet and red. Psychologists believe that to sleep in a pink room will leave you in a good, optimistic frame of mind.

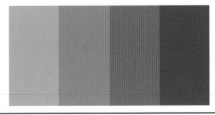

SOOTHING

Aqua

Aqua is a color derived by the mixing together of blue and green. It is on the cooler side of the color wheel, which means that it recedes in a room, creating the feeling of space and depth. Aqua is a versatile color with a gentle cleansing ambience and, with its connotations of water, it creates a soothing atmosphere, perfect for the bedroom.

pleasing and easy to achieve, the very qualities they possess that make them harmonious may also make them monotonous. So it is important to enliven the color scheme with suggestions of complementary color.

CHOOSING COLORS

At an early age peer pressure can influence color choice. For example, we are taught from an early age to see red for danger, black for sadness, white for innocence, pink for a girl and blue for a boy. Adults' color preferences can be dramatically controlled by rules of conformity, society and by individual experiences.

Like everything else, paint colors are subject to fashion fads. Just as clothes designers change their color range each year, so do the fabric and wallpaper design houses. This puts pressure on paint manufacturers to keep up with current trends. Thus, each year, more and more subtle shades are added to paint ranges. Consumers can only benefit from the wider choice, but it does make the task of choosing colors all the harder.

There are some color combinations, however, that never seem to fall prey to fashion, and these go on evolving through the years, still managing to look new and exciting; blue and yellow, or the classic neutral range are obvious examples. But for some, the idea of using a color that has been used before is not appealing; the yearning for originality and inspiration is too strong to suppress.

EFFECT OF LIGHTING

Before choosing colors for your bedroom, check the quality of

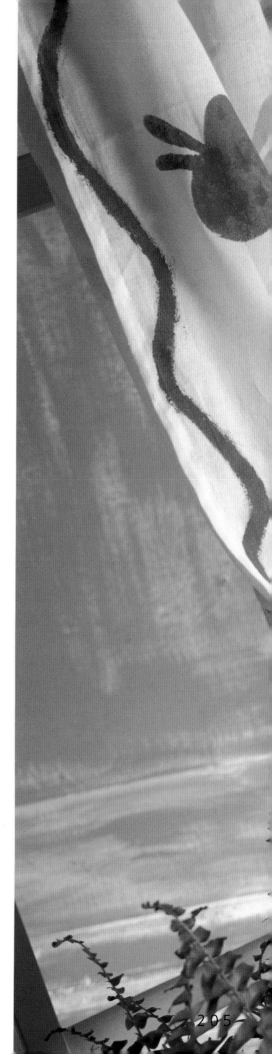

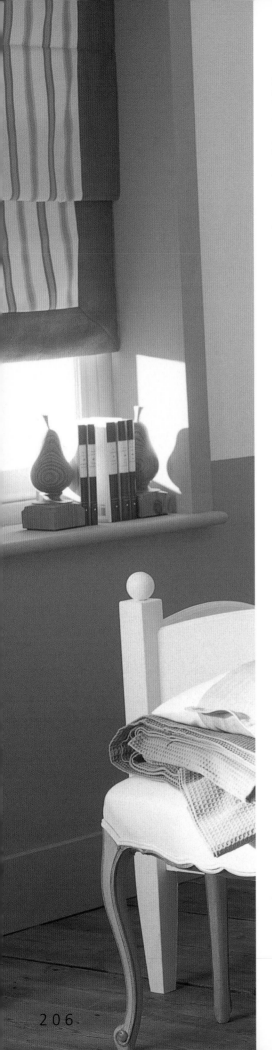

natural light your room receives. In sunlight, colors usually take a stronger or deeper tone than in poor natural light. In a bedroom that has poor natural light you might do well to choose pale colors for your decorating scheme as they will reflect light back into the room rather than absorb it. Determine the general direction from which the light is entering the room, as this may alter at different times of the day. A room that faces due south and so is a little dull in the mornings might induce you to brighten it up by painting the walls a sunny yellow; this could send you racing for your sunglasses in the afternoon when the room is flooded in natural sunlight. One solution is to opt for colors and tones that work well in both artificial and natural light.

CREATING ATMOSPHERE

Another aspect to consider is the atmosphere you want to create in your bedroom. Dark and warm colors can make a room cosy and more intimate, but they can also make the room appear smaller. Red, orange, yellow and pink are generally described as advancing colors, that is, they appear to come towards you when applied to the wall. Warm colors are good to use in cool south-facing rooms, as they provide a feeling of warmth and create cosy interiors. Light, cool colors, on the other hand, can create a feeling of space and airiness. Blue, white and green are cool colors; use them in a north-facing room to create a fresh, calm scheme.

APPLE
Green

Green is a good natural color, varying in hue from citrus lime to sage, and is found on the cool side of the color wheel. It can look dramatic when partnered by red or by orange. For a more harmonious combination, use blue and yellow. Green also works well with the pale natural range, like vanilla and linen.

All the room makeovers featured in this section have a strong individual atmosphere which was purposely created by the careful use of color, furnishings and accessories: in the terracotta room, the atmosphere derived from the memory of a Greek holiday; in the Matisse room, a painting dictated the use of sunny colors and roughly painted walls.

Atmosphere, however, is dependent not just on color but on texture as well. When it comes to choosing paint, there are many options available: satin, gloss, semi gloss and low sheen are all available in acrylic water-based paint, as well as some alkyd paint. With the introduction of acrylic water-based varnish, glazes can be mixed up easily; these give an extra dimension of texture to a room when applied over plain white walls.

TESTING COLORS

It is a good idea to do as much research as you can before actually commencing your decorating. If you intend to use a fabric either for blinds or curtains, then your color choice should reflect that. Perhaps this could be your starting point or color reference. Always take a small piece of your chosen fabric or wallpaper with you when choosing either paint or accessories; don't rely on your memory, as it will undoubtedly let you down. Try to access as many of the design houses as you can. Treat yourself to a few of the interior magazines readily available in your corner store. And when you feel that you have

TRANQUIL
Blue

True moody blue is a timeless favorite. It is the supreme cool color, evoking a sense of tranquility. Blue's rich and varied tones are endless. Deep intense blues can give an energetic and fresh feel to a room, adding depth and contrast. Pale, subtle and muted shades of blue can create the feel of open, airy spaces.

seen as much as you need to, go to your nearest paint supplier and collect a range of paint swatches. Don't be afraid to take as many different tones of your color choice away with you as you like —they are there specifically for that purpose. Invariably the tones of color will change in your own environment. Color changes when it is compared to and against its opposite. For example green will look far greener when next to the redder tones. Blue will look more blue when it is next to pink as they harmonize together.

Try out a few of your chosen paint effects on sheets of lining paper. This will give you a realistic sense of the color and the opportunity of perfecting the paint effect you are going to achieve. You can then pin these up in your bedroom and live with them for a while, observing how light changes the color. Sometimes it is not the immediate impact that you desire; alternatively, the more subtle effect may merge too far into the background when lived with for a time. This will also offer you the

SUNSHINE
Yellow

Yellow is the most cheerful of colors. Its bright light-reflecting quality cannot help but lift your spirits. Yellow is warm and will bring a source of light to even the darkest of rooms. Its tonal range travels from citrus lemon through to sultry yellow ochre, with sunny and muted shades in between. Yellow works well with blue, purple and green.

CALMING
Lavender

This beautiful atmospheric color sits on the color wheel between the two primary colors of blue and red. Because of the mix of warm and cool tones, there is a great balance within lavender's shade. You can either create a warm pinky lavender, or a violet tone, which will recede. Use it especially with green, pink or orange.

opportunity to see how the light changes throughout the day. This may take time and will require patience, but it will help to create the look that is right for you.

EXISTING FURNITURE
Very few people are in the happy position of starting from scratch with an unlimited budget and no commitments to a few inherited heirlooms or granny's rosewood wardrobe. If you do have to work around inherited objects, do this in a positive way and make the room work around them. Perhaps you could use a color indicated in a chair covering as the basis of your decorating scheme. If you really feel the need to change your decor and these items simply do not fit into the new color scheme, there is always the possibility of re-upholstering, stripping or painting the pieces to match your room. Whatever you decide, don't ignore these items in your color scheme, and pretend that they do not belong in your room, as the result will be one of incoherence and disappointment.

The deliciously inspiring combination of subtle ice cream shades used in this decorating scheme creates a peaceful haven.

Pastel Shades

These subtle pastel shades of raspberry pink, blue, lilac, vanilla and mint green complement one another beautifully and the combination of them is deliciously inspiring. The harmonious blend of light and air creates a peaceful and relaxed space.

There is a huge variety of ice cream colors to choose from for your room scheme. As these pastel colors have the same creamy and chalky hue, it is possible to use a large number of them in the same room. This is normally inadvisable as one

PROJECTS FROM
THIS MAKEOVER
SHOW YOU:

• *How to dry-brush a wall*

• *How to revamp an iron
bed frame*

• *How to make a bedspread
curtain and tie back*

211

color can react against another, giving an overall inconsistency; however, in this case, the tonal range blends and shimmers together, with no one color dominating, and each color adding to the other's natural vibrance. The balance between warm and cool colors is broken only by the addition of accessories in slightly deeper tones; the furniture painted in a soft mid tone of lilac reaffirms the importance of color equality. When using more than one color in a room, give each color the same amount of space. To create a balanced feel to the color, you must use colors of similar intensity. The lack of pattern in the room helps to maintain the clean uncluttered feel.

PREPARATION

Make sure that all holes in the ceiling or walls are filled with general all-purpose spackling compound, and that any loose wallpaper is stuck down fast with wallpaper paste. Any slight indentations will show up more after the surface is decorated. Protect any furnishings that cannot be removed with dust sheets; cover the floor, too, as splashes and drips will inevitably land there.

Mix the glazes, ensuring that you have the right amount required. You will need a clean mixing pail, acrylic clear varnish and a small quantity of the paint in the color you want to apply. For each color glaze you will need 1 part water-based paint to 2 parts varnish. You can mix the glaze with a spatula; if, however, the quantity you require is great, use a paint paddle attached to an electric drill, to make mixing easier. Before applying glaze, mask off any adjoining surfaces with low-tack masking tape, as this will help to create clean lines.

DRY-BRUSHING

This technique is easy to achieve and results in a subtle broken paint effect which is perfect for pale paint colors, and also more suitable for this room scheme than a flat coat of water-based paint.

EXPERT TIP

- *If the paint starts to flake when drying, it probably means that you have used water-based paint over an alkyd-based paint, such as gloss. Before painting with acrylic, prepare the surface first by rubbing it down with sandpaper and applying a good coat of acrylic all-purpose primer.*

1 Using a household brush, apply a coat of vanilla water-based paint over the surface to cover it entirely. Allow to dry.

2 Wrap sandpaper around a block of wood and use this to rub over the painted surface. This smooths the surface in readiness for the top coat of paint.

3 Mix up a glaze with 1 part pink acrylic to 2 parts acrylic varnish. Dip a household brush in the glaze, then brush it over the surface in long vertical strokes. This effect allows the brush-strokes and part of the base coat to remain visible. Allow to dry.

Revamping an iron bed frame

MATERIALS

- cast iron bed frame
- bowl
- rubber gloves
- cloth or scrubbing brush
- coarse-grade sandpaper
- household paintbrush
- all-purpose acrylic primer or anti-rust primer
- water-based paint: white, pink, pistachio
- fine artist's brush
- soft cloth
- medium-grade sandpaper
- raw umber paint pigment
- acrylic clear varnish
- dragging brush
- silver metallic paint

You might think that it is all very well being tempted to buy an old jug from a junk shop, because you know that prior to it taking up pride of place on your dresser it will meet with a thorough wash or a keen dusting down. However, if the piece you intend to purchase is likely to be the weight of a small cart horse and rusty as well, the idea of cleaning such a large object might not be so appealing. However, this project shows that with a little determination and some elbow grease, it is quite possible to rescue and revamp a large cast iron bed frame, thus combining the elegance of an age gone by with the comfort and convenience of today's lifestyle.

1 Before being able to tackle the rot or damage to a cast iron bed frame you need to remove all the surface dust and dirt. Fill a large bowl with warm soapy water and use a cloth to wash away as much of the loose paintwork as you can; alternatively, a stiff scrubbing brush will help with this.

2 Allow the bed frame to dry, then rub it vigorously with coarse-grade sandpaper to remove any remaining rust and old paintwork.

3 Using a household paintbrush, apply a coat of all-purpose acrylic primer over the entire bed frame. Alternatively, if there is rust present on the frame, use anti-rust primer instead. Allow to dry.

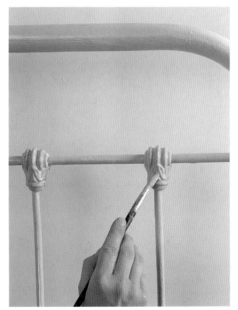

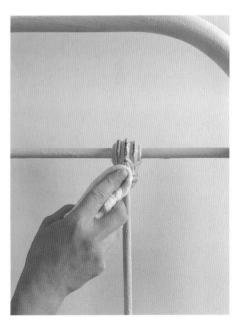

4 Paint a coat of white water-based paint over the whole bed frame, watching out for any runs or drips. Leave to dry, then, if necessary, apply a second coat for an even all-over coverage.

5 Using a fine artist's brush, paint any details or features of the bed in pink water-based paint.

6 Using a soft cloth, rub away some of the paint on the details to create the look of wear and tear.

7 Paint fine lines of pistachio-colored water-based paint over the details to highlight the intricate metalwork. Allow the paint to dry thoroughly.

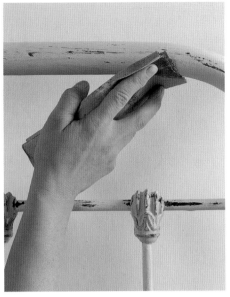

8 Using medium-grade sandpaper, rub down the paintwork on the bed frame to reveal patches of previous paint layers, and in some areas bare metal. This will add to the aged and worn feel that an old bed would almost certainly have.

9 Make some ageing glaze by mixing a tablespoon of raw umber paint pigment in a pot of acrylic varnish. Brush a coat of ageing glaze over the frame using a long-haired soft dragging brush. Allow the glaze to pool in some areas, but do not allow any runs to occur.

10 Using a fine artist's brush, apply silver metallic paint to any intricate moldings to highlight and accentuate these areas. Allow to dry.

MATERIALS
- padded bedspread
- sewing thread
- sewing machine
- tape measure
- silk flowers
- ribbons for tie back
- dressmaking scissors
- pins
- 2 brass rings
- pencil
- bradawl
- hanging hook
- nail
- hammer

Bedspread curtain and tie back

In this project, a simple curtain is created from a bedspread, while pretty ribbons and silk flowers, normally used for decorating hats, are used in an unusual decoration for a curtain tie back. In this pale room, which is continually flooded with light, the window dressing needed to be simple but also to effectively exclude light. The solution came in the shape of a soft quilted antique bedspread which was double-sided with padding in between, therefore negating the need to line or interline. The bedspread was cream on one side and a soft pink appliqué on the other, so when the top was folded over to create a loop to feed onto the curtain pole, there was an instant design. A simple ribbon tie back to hold back the quilt curtain for daytime use allows a glimpse of the decorative silk flowers.

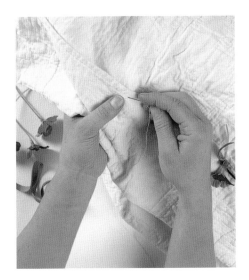

1 Fold over the top of the bedspread to make a loop of fabric that the curtain pole can be slipped through. Baste the fabric layers then machine stitch to secure. At measured intervals, handstitch the silk flowers and ribbons to the bedspread top.

2 Calculate the length of tie back you will need. Measure the distance from where you will position the hook on the wall around the curtain and back to the hook again. Then cut the length of ribbon accordingly. If your chosen ribbon is thin, back it with a more robust one. Lay the ribbon flat and pin the narrower ribbon on the top and machine sew around the edge. Tie a large bow in the center of the ribbon. Stitch the silk flowers into position on one side of the ribbon.

3 Attach a brass ring to each side of the tie back. Fold each ribbon end by 12 mm (½ in). Lay the ring on the folded end, fold back the ribbon to enclose the ring. Then stitch the ribbon to secure.

4 Position the tie back around the curtain and mark with a pencil cross on the wall the position of the tie back hook. Using a bradawl, make a small dent in the wall in the center of the cross.

5 Attach the hanging hook to the wall by carefully tapping a nail through the hole in the hook. Then simply slip the tie back rings over the hook to hold back the curtain.

Lemon 'n' Lime

This sunny color scheme of lemon and lime is fresh, clean, youthful and invigorating. In this bedroom, you will want to leap out of bed in the mornings, full of vitality and enthusiasm for the day ahead.

Although paint has miraculous transforming abilities, sometimes the desire to use a much-loved wallpaper is just too tempting, and this combination of lemon and lime checks has always been a favorite. Many home decorators are reluctant to attempt to hang their own wallpaper.

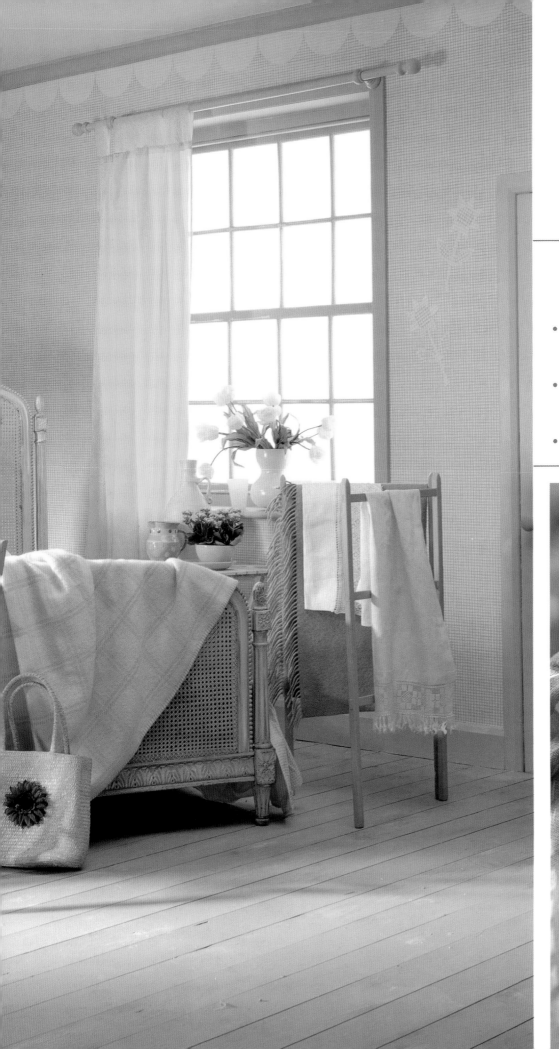

But if care is taken and a methodical approach is followed, there is no reason why anyone should be discouraged.

In this room two different colorways of the same wallpaper were used. The checked paper is available in lemon and lime: the lemon was used on the ceiling and the lime on the walls. The cornice was dragged in a deep lime green and the woodwork was painted in turquoise. The window and door moldings were painted light lime green. The bed was dragged in pale lemon and the table and clothes dryer were painted turquoise. The accessories picked up on the checks and lemon and lime scheme.

PREPARATION

Before wallpapering your room, remove the old wallpaper and make good any damage done to the wall surface in so doing. Treat any damp patches, as failure to deal with it at this stage will be expensive if the staining appears later through the new wallpaper.

Use prepasted paper or paste lining paper on the walls prior to hanging wallpaper. This should be pasted on horizontally rather than vertically; this evens out any odd lumps and bulges in the wall, and prevents them showing through the wallpaper for an uneven finish.

HANGING WALLPAPER

Take your time when hanging wallpaper for the first time. Although it may look easy, achieving a neat finish with patterns matching and no trapped air bubbles takes a bit of planning and care. Unroll the wallpaper and measure out your required length; do not underestimate the drop. If you intend to use striped wallpaper, it is crucial that the first piece is hung vertically straight.

1 Ensure that the wallpaper pattern is both vertically and horizontally correct. Brush wallpaper paste over the back of the wallpaper. Place the wallpaper on to the prepared wall surface. Then, using a dry, clean brush and applying gentle downward pressure, stroke the wallpaper smoothly into position. Brush out any air bubbles that are trapped between the wall and the paper.

2 Where the wallpaper meets and overhangs the skirting board, gently push the wallpaper into the corner to make a neat, straight fold. Using the wallpaper shears, carefully score along the folded edge to enable you to trim away the excess wallpaper.

3 Gently peel back the wallpaper at the base and, using the shears, cut cleanly along the scored line. Take care not to leave any ragged edges or rip the paper. Either discard the excess wallpaper, or put it to one side for making wallpaper scallops (see page 222).

4 Using the dry papering brush, push the wallpaper back against the wall. Gently scrub the paper into the corner with the edge of the brush. Using a soft damp cloth, wipe away any residue of paste that may be left on either the wallpaper or the skirting board.

MATERIALS
• dinner plate
• wallpaper
• masking tape
• pencil
• cutting mat or cardboard
• craft knife
• saucer
• pinking shears
• wallpaper paste

Making scallops and wallpaper decoration

This project uses leftover pieces of wallpaper to create a border of scallops along the base of the cornice, and flower motifs around the window, to add to the decorative feel of the room. As well as involving little or no outlay, these ideas can be used to liven up a piece of furniture, or to make your own border or dado.

1 To create a scalloped border from wallpaper, place a dinner plate over the edge of a piece of wallpaper so that it is half on the paper. Mark the halfway point on each side of the plate with a strip of masking tape. Draw around the curved plate with a pencil. Continue to draw scalloped curves along the paper, always lining up the edge of the paper with the masking tape on the plate.

2 Place a cutting mat or piece of cardboard under the wallpaper to protect your work surface. Using a craft knife, carefully cut along the penciled curves to create a row of scallops, ensuring that you do not cut through to the edge of the wallpaper. The scalloped border can now be pasted directly under the cornice.

3 Find two circular objects you can draw around; one should be larger than the other. Here we have used a saucer and a reel of masking tape. Draw around the saucer on lemon-checked wallpaper. This circle will form the basis of the flowerhead.

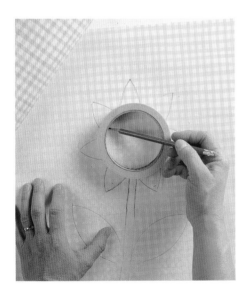

4 Draw a simple flower shape. The petals should extend no further than the original circle. Add a stalk and a pair of leaves. Then place the masking tape in the center and draw around it. Place the tape on green-checked wallpaper. Draw round the inside of it.

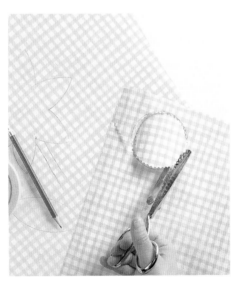

5 Using pinking shears to create an appliquéd effect, cut out the center section of the flower motif, and the rest of the flower motif from the lemon-checked wallpaper.

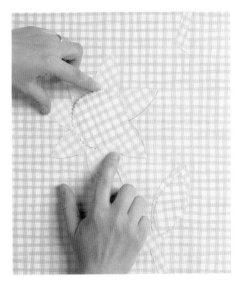

6 Using wallpaper paste, stick the flower design on to the wall, pressing it from the center outward to remove air bubbles. Cut smaller leaves from the green-checked paper and stick these on top of the yellow leaves. Repeat the process for further flower motifs.

Frosting glassware

MATERIALS
- glassware
- soft cloth
- methylated spirits
- masking tape
- sponge
- white water-based paint
- acrylic clear varnish
- yellow artist's color
- blue artist's color
- stippling brush
- fine pointed soft brush
- acrylic spray varnish

Decorating glassware with this frosting technique is a quick and easy way to transform ordinary glass jugs or bowls into ornamental pieces for your home. Using little more than a tin of flat water-based paint and some acrylic varnish, you will be able to frost your glassware to match your decor. Once you have tried the following few simple steps, you can go on to design your own exciting patterns.

1 Wash the glass object thoroughly in hot soapy water, then rinse under the hot tap. Allow to dry completely and then wipe the whole surface with a clean soft cloth and methylated spirits to remove any remaining grease. Using masking tape, mask off any area that you want to remain as clear glass.

2 Dip a small piece of sponge into white water-based paint, then dab the sponge lightly all over the surface of the unmasked glass to achieve an even covering. Allow to dry completely.

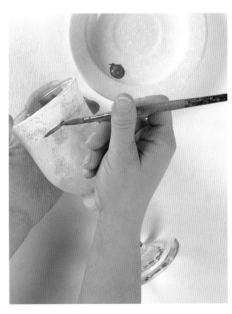

3 Mix up a glaze using a small quantity of acrylic varnish and a blob of yellow artist's color. Then, using a stippling brush, jab the glaze over the top of the dry paint on the glass. Leave to dry completely.

4 Gently peel away the masking tape. Then sponge a white base coat over the clear glass and, when dry, stipple over a complementary color glaze as shown in step 3. Alternatively, you can leave the glass clear.

5 Allow the paint to dry completely. Using a fine pointed soft brush, add further details over the top of the stippled paint in blue artist's color, covering the join of the two contrasting colors. Allow to dry, then spray the glass with clear varnish for protection.

This combination of deep blues creates a turbulent stormy atmosphere which is softened by the use of white as an accent color.

Moody Blues

The range of different blues used in this color scheme create a slightly turbulent light, giving the room a moody, atmospheric quality. The addition of white in the color scheme softens and freshens the overall feel.

Blue is a very popular color for bedrooms; we may all like our beds to be warm but on the whole we like the actual room to be cool. With the invention of central heating, the use of blue in decorating schemes has increased. The inspiration

PROJECTS FROM
THIS MAKEOVER
SHOW YOU:

• *How to paint adjoining*
  surfaces

• *How to paint a floor*

• *How to decorate ceramics*

229

for this room emerged from waking in the night to catch the last of the rolling thunder, when flashes of electric blue light streaked into the room. There is the most amazing sense of calm after a storm. This makeover is an attempt to regain that feeling of exhilaration.

As blue is a receding color, seeming to create space, you can apply the paint flat without the fear of reflective intensity. In this room the walls and ceiling were painted a warm mid-blue, the window and door a deep cobalt blue, and the woodwork a mid-lavender blue. The cornice was painted slightly unevenly in a pale lilac blue, while the floor was given a distressed finish using a cool sea-blue.

PREPARATION

Stick down any loose wallpaper with wallpaper paste, and fill any cracks in the plaster with spackling compound. As the room will be painted with flat water-based paint, pay particular attention to the condition of the walls. Make sure that they are thoroughly rubbed down and smoothed prior to painting, otherwise imperfections will show up clearly. When painting with different blues, ensure that the colors do not overlap; careful masking is essential.

Choose your accessories for the bedroom carefully. In this room, white was used together with punchy checked fabrics which are widely available in stores. They add a warming sense of welcome to what could be an austere environment.

PAINTING ADJOINING SURFACES

When painting a cornice in a different color to the ceiling and walls, it is essential to mask off the surfaces on either side of it. This will ensure that paint does not spatter on the ceiling or wall, and that the painted edges of the cornice are straight and even. Choose a color of paint that works well with the adjoining surfaces to avoid clashing. Here, the cornice is painted in pale lilac blue while the adjoining walls are painted in mid blue.

1 Stick lengths of low-tack masking tape along the edges of the ceiling and wall adjoining the cornice.

2 Using a household brush, paint the cornice with pale lilac-blue water-based paint, ensuring that the brushstrokes are confined within the lengths of masking tape to produce a clean straight edge. Allow the paint to dry thoroughly.

3 Remove the masking tape and re-apply it on the painted cornice, butting it up to the edge of the wall. Then apply mid-blue water-based paint on the wall right up to the cornice to produce a clean straight edge with no overlapping of color.

Painting a floor

MATERIALS
- hammer
- coarse-grade sandpaper
- acrylic all-purpose primer
- household brushes
- water-based paint: pink, sea-blue, creamy yellow
- large soft brush
- floor varnish

Floor painting can be the ideal answer to matching up a variety of paint colors in a room. It also lends itself to a wide and varied choice of application. There is a huge range of commercial colors available; alternatively, colors can be hand-mixed with limitless possibilities. Colors can be laid on top of one another to build up different decorative effects. Any number of designs can be used to enhance or contrast with your already existing color theme. A new floor can be antiqued or an old one brought up to date. With the use of contemporary floor varnishes widely available, there is no reason why your painted floor should not last forever.

1 Inspect the floorboards before you begin and hammer down any prominent nail heads. Then rub the floor vigorously with coarse-grade sandpaper wrapped around a block of wood to create a smooth surface. Pay particular attention to boards that are warped or split. Paint the floor with acrylic all-purpose primer and allow to dry.

2 Using a household brush, apply a base coat of pink water-based paint over the floorboards, dragging the brush over the surface to produce long brushstrokes. Allow to dry.

3 Dip a large soft brush into sea-blue water-based paint, then drag it over the base coat, allowing some of the pink to show through. Leave to dry.

4 Using a smaller household brush, apply creamy yellow water-based paint sporadically along the floorboards, carefully following the line of the grain and the previous brushmarks.

5 When the paint is thoroughly dry, apply two coats of hardwearing floor varnish to seal and protect the aged and distressed floor. Allow the first coat to dry before applying the second. Leave the varnish to dry completely before walking on the floor.

Painting ceramics

When you change the color scheme of your bedroom, and go to the trouble of finding new fabrics and lighting, it is often not possible to re-use existing accessories because they just do not match the new scheme. This project gives you a chance to redesign or change in as dramatic a way as you like any of those favorite jugs, bowls, cups and saucers that do not fit in with your decor. Painting ceramics is both inexpensive and satisfying to do as it recycles old ceramics as well as providing an excuse to vent your artistic skills, however limited they might be. In these examples artistic flair is quite unnecessary, as using masking tape makes it easy to add decorative stripes and checks to transform plain ceramics instantly.

EXPERT TIPS

- *Paint effects such as sponging or dragging can work well on ceramics when they are combined with masking or stencilling.*

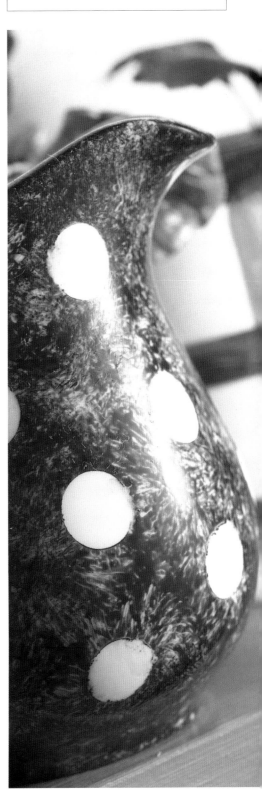

1 Wash the ceramic piece and make sure that your hands are clean and free of grease; any grease on the ceramic piece will result in the paint being repelled. Dry the ceramic piece thoroughly. For a checked design, stick lengths of masking tape in vertical stripes around the side of your ceramic piece, leaving a gap of approximately 12 mm (½ in) between each length.

2 Using a pointed artist's brush, apply mid-blue ceramic paint over the unmasked areas. Allow to dry, then peel off the masking tape. Remask the ceramic piece with horizontal bands (this time low-tack tape), again leaving 12 mm (½ in) between each band. Paint darker blue ceramic paint over the unmasked areas. Clean off any over-spills of paint with solvent and a cotton bud.

3 Allow the paint to dry, then peel off the masking tape carefully. If any paint pulls off, apply a few dabs of paint over the top to repair the damage.

4 To create a spotted design, place paper dots randomly over the piece. Stipple ceramic paint on to the surface to cover it completely. Leave to dry, then carefully peel off the paper dots to reveal clean white ceramic spots underneath. Clean off any unwanted glaze using a cotton bud. If desired, you can paint in the white dots with a contrasting color.

235

This warming terracotta decorating scheme evokes sunlight and heat and baked earth, making the bedroom very warm and cosy.

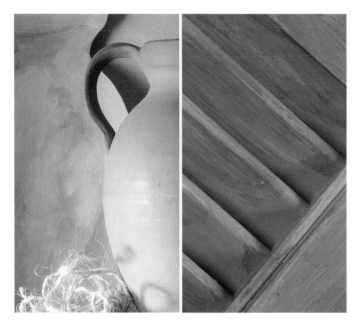

Rich Terracotta

Terracotta evokes sunlight and heat, and the rich terracotta walls in this color scheme create a warm, cosy atmosphere, ideal for a bedroom. The blue floorboards complement the walls, and soften the effect of the terracotta.

Terracotta is a very popular color, perhaps because it evokes those exotic warm countries where terracotta is so often used and where you can see and appreciate the wonderful effect and depth that the use of this rich warm color can

PROJECTS FROM
THIS MAKEOVER
SHOW YOU:

- *How to dry-brush and age surfaces*
- *How to make a découpaged trompe-l'oeil jug*
- *How to antique wooden shutters*

237

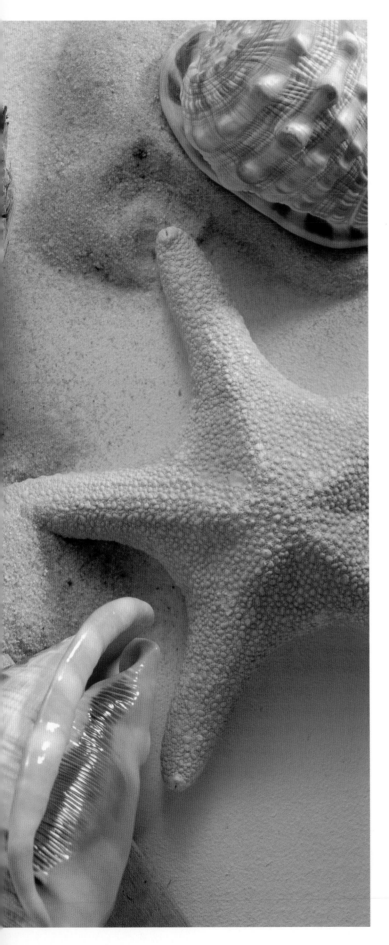

offer. Collect a few old terracotta pots together and examine their colors; you will see that terracotta is actually composed of a range of brownish-orange colors. Use a few colors and blend them together.

As the walls were the dominant part of this room, they were decorated with a terracotta colorwash. A colorwash imitates the appearance of old-fashioned, distemper-painted walls, and this paint effect gives the room a sunny, bleached atmosphere, exactly what was wanted in this texture-rich natural interior. Colorwashing is an easy technique to do and quite a useful technique if the wall surface is at all lumpy or irregular.

PREPARATION

When colorwashing, lots of liquid may be splashed around the room, so make sure that any furnishings that cannot be removed are covered with both dust sheets and polythene to protect them from staining. Also ensure that any electrical outlets, such as sockets, are switched off, the plugs removed, and the outlets covered in polythene and sealed with masking tape.

If the walls are in good decorative order and are already either painted white or another suitable tone, then all that is required is to give the walls a good wash with a sponge and a bowl of warm water. This should remove any dirt and dust. If there are any greasy patches, remove them with a general household cleaner prior to colorwashing.

If the walls are a dark color, they will require priming prior to being color-washed. If drips and runs occur when priming, and these cannot be blended in using a clean damp brush, allow the area to dry completely then re-prime, taking care to blend the primer at the edges. This should help disguise the area and diffuse any darker patches.

DRY-BRUSHING AND AGEING

These techniques are easy to do following the steps below. They are also useful when decorating woodwork as they add depth and texture to what would otherwise be areas of flat color.

1 Mask off the wall and floor on either side of the surface to be painted. Mix a wash using 1 part pale gray water-based paint and 3 parts acrylic clear varnish, then add a little water until the mixture is like milk. Apply a base coat of the pale gray wash.

2 Allow the base coat to dry. Then dip a dry brush into deeper gray water-based paint and drag this over the base coat, allowing streaks of the pale gray to show through. Leave to dry.

3 Mix ageing glaze by adding a small amount of burnt umber pigment to acrylic clear varnish. Add more pigment as required to achieve the desired depth of tone. Brush the ageing glaze over the painted surface and leave to dry.

Découpaged jug

Découpage is the cutting out and sticking down of paper decoration, and it is a good alternative to stencilling. This project shows how to make a paper terracotta jug to use as a trompe-l'oeil decoration on a bedroom wall. You can either stick or simply lean your flat jug against the wall to create a piece of decorative fun.

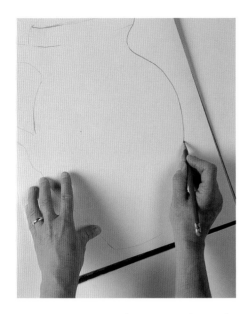

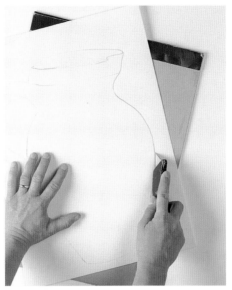

1 Paint a piece of paper with acrylic all-purpose primer; paper will discolor if left unprotected, so a coat of primer will not only help to prevent damage but will also make a good surface to work on. Then, using a pencil, draw or trace the outline of your image on the paper.

2 Place the paper on a cutting mat or piece of cardboard to protect the underlying work surface. Then, using a craft knife, carefully cut out the penciled shape, working slowly and turning the paper as you go to retain the soft curves of the design.

3 Mix up a dilute wash of 1 part terracotta paint to 3 parts acrylic clear varnish. When mixed thoroughly, add a little water until the mixture is the consistency of milk. Using an artist's brush, paint the cut-out jug with the terracotta wash to establish a three-dimensional effect.

4 Using a finer artist's brush, add patches of brown and green water-based paint to shade the sides of the jug, highlight the rim and emphasize the jug's curved shape. Keep stepping back from the image to judge the effect, correcting any details as necessary as you are painting.

5 Allow the paint to dry, then apply a coat of acrylic clear varnish over the top to protect the image. Allow the découpaged jug to dry flat.

MATERIALS

- wooden shutters
- fine-grade sandpaper
- cloth
- household paintbrush
- terracotta low sheen paint
- coarse-grade sandpaper
- fine artist's brush
- gray water-based paint
- burnt umber acrylic paint
- satin finish acrylic clear
- varnish

Antiquing wooden shutters

Aged and antiqued wooden shutters immediately create a look that is reminiscent of foreign holidays and exciting times. When used in a room like this, they add a distinct air of authenticity. Sometimes shutters are preferable for a window for practical reasons, for instance in a bathroom with a large sash window to the front, where partial privacy is required. Shutters can offer the same privacy, warmth and light control as other more traditional forms of window dressing, but at the same time they create a more unusual architectural finish. Antiquing shutters is a simple and effective way of linking a decorating theme such as the Mediterranean, sunsoaked feel of this room. The following step-by-step guide shows you how to set about antiquing a pair of shutters.

- *To avoid drips when painting shutters, work with as dry a brush as possible; do not overload the brush with paint. Turn the shutter as you are applying paint as this gives you an opportunity to catch and disperse any runs as they occur.*

- *When applying the final ageing glaze, it is better to apply two or three lighter coats of glaze rather than one heavy brown coat, which can be the result of over-zealous quantities of burnt umber being added to the initial glaze.*

1 Rub the shutters lightly with fine-grade sandpaper, then wipe them over with a damp cloth to remove any dust. Using a household paintbrush, apply a coat of terracotta low sheen paint over each shutter, taking care to catch any drips or runs. Check that as the paint is applied to one side of the louvers that no paint is pooling on the other side.

2 When the paint is completely dry—usually two hours or so—rub the shutters vigorously with coarse-grade sandpaper, turning the shutters as you work to give an even feel. Then rub the edges of the shutter frame with sandpaper to remove sections of paint completely; this will create an impression of natural wear and tear.

3 With a fine artist's brush, apply patches of gray water-based paint to the heavily sanded areas and rub this in with your finger. This will create the effect of old wood under the terracotta paintwork. Then continue to sand and scrape at the paint until a satisfactory look is achieved.

4 Mix up some ageing glaze by adding a blob of burnt umber acrylic paint to a tin of satin finish acrylic varnish and mixing thoroughly. Apply this in sweeping brushstrokes across the louvers and around the frame in an anti-clockwise direction. Allow to dry, then apply a coat of acrylic varnish for protection.

MAKEOVER PROJECT

This muted mix of soft cream, vanilla and pale gray
creates an effect of elegance and sophistication, which
is ideal for a bedroom.

Neutral Tones

The muted tones of cream, vanilla and pale sultry
gray featured in this decorating scheme, balanced
with the simplicity and understatement of the
furnishings, have created an effect of elegance
and sophistication. This is a bedroom to lounge
around in wearing sheer silk pajamas, should you
have the inclination.

The inspiration for this room evolved from many
sources: old French novels and films, antique
cotton lace sheets, a small ceramic cherub rescued

PROJECTS FROM
THIS MAKEOVER
SHOW YOU:

• *How to sponge a wall*

• *How to antique a table*

• *how to make a fabric*

lampshade

245

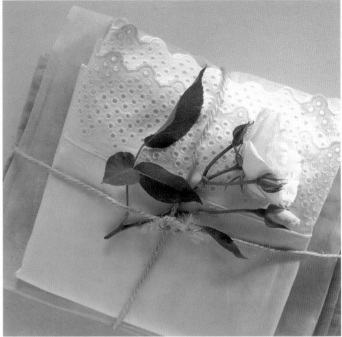

from a flea market, and a soft white rose still glistening with dew. When these objects were collected together, a paint color card was consulted and the choice of soft shades of vanilla, lily white, cream and pale gray emerged. It also became obvious that part of the attraction of these inspirational objects was their time-worn appearance, and so it was important that this was also reflected in the room, to create the impression of faded elegance.

The paint was applied using different techniques, thus avoiding any hard edges or defining lines. Subtle tones of color were used and no aspect of the room was overstated. The effect is a soft blending of colors.

PREPARATION

Before you begin to paint, go over the ceiling, walls and woodwork to check for peeling paper, air bubbles and any cracks. Stick any loose paper back in position with wallpaper paste. Cut any air bubbles and stick back in position with paste. This is especially important for ceilings; if loose paper is painted over, the weight of the wet paint might cause it to tear and fall, and bring with it a section of ceiling plaster. Fill in any cracks with all-purpose spackling compound, allow to dry, then sand to a smooth finish. This preparation is essential to ensure a smooth finish.

Prepare your paint colors in readiness for using them. The use of neutral colors has always been popular; pale tones can be a sound starting point for adding extra color, which can be gently added at any stage.

SPONGING A WALL

Before sponging a wall, you must first prime it with acrylic all-purpose primer. This seals the surface and provides a good surface on which to apply glaze. If the surface is not sealed, the glaze will soak into the wall and spoil the effect. In this makeover, the walls and ceiling were delicately sponged in a pale vanilla and acrylic glaze over a white primed surface.

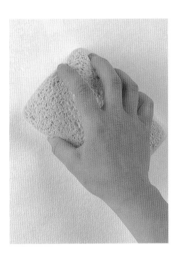

1 Using a household brush, paint the wall surface with acrylic all-purpose primer. Apply the primer in all directions, up and down, side to side and diagonally so that brushmarks are not visible. Ensure the coverage is even. Allow to dry.

2 In a pot, mix together 1 part pale vanilla water-based paint with 2 parts acrylic varnish. Use a paint-brush to stir the mixture together well; this is the sponging glaze.

3 Dip a sponge lightly into the vanilla glaze, then dab the sponge on the wall to create a pattern of small dots. Continue to dab the sponge over the surface, dipping it into the glaze as needed, until the entire wall is covered in a soft, mottled paint effect.

Antiquing a table

The effect of antiquing produces and imitates the effects of time on paint and adds a worn look to the newest of pieces, allowing for a mellow blend between genuinely old and new. This small pine occasional table was transformed into a delightful piece which, when intermingled with other genuine antiques in the room, adds a degree of elegance and charm. It also has the added advantage of being user-friendly and, because of the acrylic varnish, knock-resistant.

1 Rub the table with sandpaper wrapped around a block to smooth the surface and give it a key to enable the paint to adhere. Then prime it with acrylic all-purpose primer to seal the surface, ensuring that the table is evenly covered. Allow to dry.

2 When the primer is thoroughly dry, rub the table lightly with sandpaper so that small patches of the original surface show through the primer.

3 Using a household brush, apply a coat of white water-based paint thinly and evenly over the entire table. Leave to dry, then sand the surface very lightly again for a smooth finish.

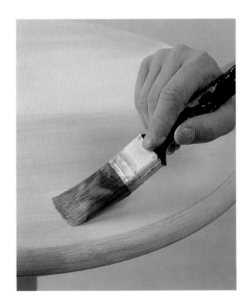

4 Mix the ageing glaze by adding a small amount of burnt umber pigment to acrylic clear varnish. Add more pigment as required to achieve the desired depth of tone. Brush the glaze over the surface of the table and leave to dry completely.

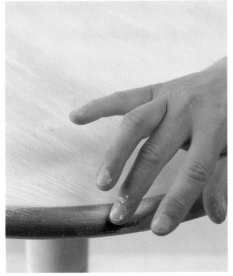

5 Dip a finger in gold paint and rub it roughly around the edge of the tabletop to imitate gilt edging. Add a further gold band around the table leg if desired. The intermittent application of the gold emulates the natural wear on the edge of the table. The end result might not fool an antiques expert but it will look authentic in a room scheme such as this.

EXPERT TIPS

- *For an authentic look, ensure the table is completely sealed with several coats of acrylic clear varnish, sanding with a fine-grade abrasive paper between each coat.*

- *If the table is to receive heavy use, cut a glass or perspex top to protect the table surface.*

249

Making a fabric lampshade

MATERIALS
- lampshade frame
- tape measure
- fabric
- dressmaking scissors
- iron
- pins
- sewing thread
- sewing machine
- tailor's chalk
- pom-pom fringing
- craft knife
- tapestry needle or safety pin
- ribbon or cord

Lighting can significantly change the ambience of any room. In this room a soft natural glow was required and this was achieved by the use of a handmade lampshade which offered both a delicate elegance and a gentle muted illumination. The basic shade can be enhanced by the use of a decorative fringe or ribbon, which can be sewn on to the edge of the skirt of the lampshade. The fabric chosen in this project was a pale fine-weave flame-retardant linen; it was gently gathered around the top of a lampshade frame and then pulled together with ribbon and allowed to hang in soft folds over the lamp base. Fringing completed the look. This lampshade is easy to make and will add a charming personal touch to any bedroom.

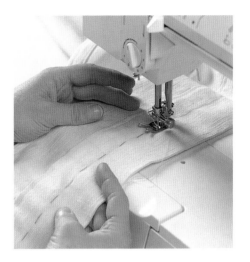

1 To calculate the amount of fabric needed for the lampshade, measure the circumference of the frame at the widest point then multiply this by two; this will give the width of fabric required. To calculate the length needed, measure the height of the lampshade frame. Then add 12 cm (4¾ in) to this to allow for turning and hemming at top and bottom.

2 Cut out the fabric with dressmaking scissors. Carefully fold over 2 cm (¾ in) of one long edge of the fabric and press with an iron. Then fold the edge over 6 cm (2⅜ in) and press again. Insert pins to secure the fold. Repeat this process at the opposite long edge of the fabric, but this time making the second fold only 2 cm (¾ in) deep.

3 Baste the two hems and, using a sewing machine, stitch the hems 3 mm (⅛ in) from each inner edge. On the wider folded edge, measure 2 cm (¾ in) from the line of hem stitches and mark this along the whole width of fabric using tailor's chalk. Baste along this chalked line, then machine stitch, finishing the threads off properly at each end.

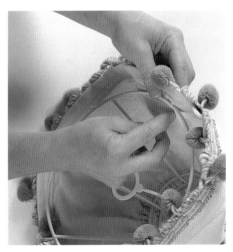

4 Lay the fabric flat so the hems are facing downward. Cut a length of pom-pom fringing to fit along the length of the lampshade. Pin this along the hemmed edge of the lampshade. Then baste and machine stitch the fringe in place along the line of hem stitches.

5 Fold the fabric in half, right sides facing, and raw edges together. Leaving a 12 mm (½ in) seam, stitch the sides together. Turn the shade right side out. Cut a slit in between the two lines of stitching in the top layer of fabric at the top of the shade. Using a tapestry needle, thread ribbon through the slit and along the channel, gathering the fabric as you go. Tie the ribbon ends.

6 Fit the lampshade frame inside the fabric shade and secure in position with large loop stitches sewn around the gathered fabric and the top wire ring of the frame. Then lift the shade and give it a gentle shake to settle the fabric in place. Stitch small looping stitches attaching the folds of fabric to the bottom ring of the frame. Attach the lampshade to the lamp base to finish.

251

BATHROOM
MAKEOVERS

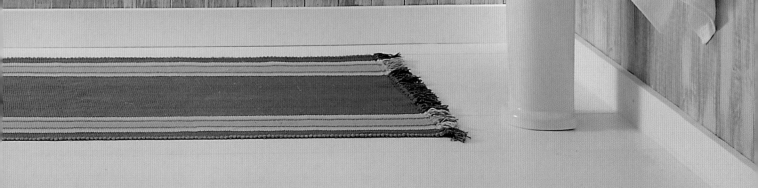

Morning; the alarm rings heralding another busy day. We snooze for ten minutes more than we really should. Then the mad dashing around the house begins, getting ready to leave in such a short space of time. The bathroom is a place of necessity at this time of day. Its purpose is purely functional. We need the bathroom to perform for us as a place in which to clean ourselves, perhaps shave or apply make up. Most of all we require that our bathroom is constantly on stand-by.

Evening; the day's work is complete – perhaps the children have been entertained, fed and put to bed or some tiring household chores have been completed. We run a warm bath and disappear into a private world for the purposes of basic hygiene but mostly for relaxation. Now the bathroom becomes a place of sanctuary and reflection.

More than any other room in the house, the bathroom is multi-functional, serving necessity as well as our requirements for luxury. It is one of the areas in a home that guests are very likely to see, and it is the only room that is likely to have only one person in it at a time. It may be the only room in the house with a lock on the door; a room in which it is permissible to spend time alone, no explanations required. No wonder so much time and effort is exerted on the decor and surroundings of the bathroom.

Bathroom decor is often a reflection of the personalities of the main residents of the home. Sometimes, it is the only room that stimulates a half description, by way of warning, before you visit: 'we allowed

ourselves to go wild in one room only, just down the hall on the right'. Intricate mosaics, a first attempt at mural painting, exotic marble paneling ... only in the bathroom! Like seeing your superiors in casual clothing for the first time, the bathroom is a great leveller.

And so, we come to your bathroom. Not only have you looked briefly at the pictures in these pages but now you sit down to read the text. Within these pages you will see pictures of the same bathroom in six differing guises. Each style has been selected to illustrate the effects that different colors can have and to show you how dramatic a transformation can be. Each room has some small projects, such as storage ideas that can of course be transported into another style of room or even used alone. Everything comes with step-by-step instructions and photographs. Where a step-by-step photograph does not show any working hands, it is either very simple and basic, described in the text below it or has been left uncluttered by hands in order to show you more clearly what is required for that particular step.

Some of the rooms look, at a glance, as though some time has been invested in the transformation. Happily, all of these bathrooms were turned around in just two days by only two people. Allow yourself two weekends and you will be able to achieve these results and take breaks to complete other essential chores.

Most of the rooms and projects are low-cost ideas and the overall effect is created by the color schemes, as opposed to the actual techniques used. Once the basic carpentry or 'making' is complete, it will take very little time to adjust or alter a chosen color if you change your mind. Remember that a coat of paint is not even 'skin deep' and can be changed in the blinking of an eye to something that appeals to you more. The projects in this section are suitable for people of all levels of DIY experience, including beginners. I encourage you to have a go because there is nothing to match the pleasure of standing back and admiring your own handiwork. When your new bathroom is complete, reward yourself by locking yourself in for as long as you need with a good book. Enjoy!

Using color in your bathroom

It is important to understand the first rule in selecting a color before moving on with the transformation of any room in the home: there are no rules. Thereafter, there are experts who will advise you or point you in the right direction, and magazines and books like this that may inspire you or give you ideas but the final decision on what color to use will always depend on your personal choice.

Because color can affect mood, and because of the special demands of the bathroom, the choice of color for this room, more than any other room in the house, is key. Can a color be trusted to be, for example, both cheering and peaceful? How can you prevent a muted 'mucky' color from looking unhygienic or dirty? Do not despair; if you like a particular color, there are ways of making it work well for you in your bathroom.

While most of us do not have the luxury of great space in the bathroom, any size of room can lend itself to a particular style, be it modern and minimal or traditional and homely. Changing the style of your bathroom completely may be costly or time-consuming so a simpler and cheaper option may be to change the colors. This can completely alter the mood of your bathroom and give you surprising and stunning results.

COLOR AT DIFFERENT TIMES OF DAY

Some shades change dramatically in artificial or evening light, compared to how they look in the day. Flat lilac can be a prime example of this, depending on the manufacturer of the paint – it looks much more pink in the evening. So much so that with some brands you may be disappointed by it. Run a simple test before deciding on a color by painting some boards with paint from a sample pot or the smallest pot that you can have mixed for you in a store. Keep them in the bathroom for a few days and see how they are affected by changing lighting conditions.

LOOKING AFTER YOUR BATHROOM

A full re-paint is not always necessary to make your bathroom look like new. Washable paints allow you to wipe the walls just as often as you wipe the surface of the tiles. Color will start to fade firstly in areas that are touched regularly, for example, the areas around the door handle and light switches. Keeping a jar of the paint in the bathroom means that you can quickly patch up an area as you notice it wearing. Rinse the brush in the basin and leave it all to dry overnight. Paints that come ready mixed from the supplier can be invaluable for this as they are usually available in tiny tester pots, which can prove very practical for small maintenance tasks. A small brush that has been used in alkyd-based paint can be washed by rubbing it over a bar of household soap.

The cords on light switches

and fabric surfaces, such as curtain tie backs, can also become grubby and will require washing or changing. Just cutting the bottom few inches off a light cord is a rapid remedy.

Most of all it is the white paint in a room that appreciates maintenance and that creates a 'clean' feeling. For this reason, use the highest quality white paint possible and study the can for information on washability. Keep some spare and re-paint white surfaces at least once a year.

Tile grout discolors over time. It can be spruced up with special paints but is best removed and re-applied. This need not be a daunting task because you can work one tile at a time, removing the old grout with a little scraper and re-applying fresh immediately. When your tiles begin to look tired, you can set about re-grouting just one or two each evening as the bath fills. The whole tiled area shown on pages 290–1 was re-grouted to look like new in just one day.

Floor grout always becomes discolored. It is also more difficult to remove and replace than wall grout. Therefore, it is advisable to use a gray or subtly colored grout so as to avoid the problems caused by discoloration from water or wear and tear.

CHOOSING LIGHTING

There are certain rules surrounding electrical appliances in bathrooms, including lighting, because of the possibility of them coming into contact with water or steam. It is therefore advisable to use the services of a professional. A mirror can be used to double

the light as it reflects and bounces back into the room. When lighting over or around a mirror, keep the light pointing at the subject that you want reflected – probably yourself, as you shave or dress. Pointing the light directly onto the surface of the mirror will make it difficult to see.

Consider also the position of ceiling lights; staring up from the bathtub into a bright light will not make for relaxation.

LIGHTING TRICKS

The bathroom lighting will have an effect on how colors look. Most artificial lighting has a yellowing effect, which can warm up the overall colors by one or two tones. Colors on the yellow side of the spectrum, such as yellows, reds and oranges have a warming effect and will make the room feel a few degrees warmer than it is. However, be aware of the fact that it will add a green edge to blues and an orange edge to colors with red in the mix, such as pinks and lavenders.

At the other end of the spectrum, blues and grays have a decidedly cooling effect. It follows, therefore, that a blue lightbulb, such as a daylight simulation bulb, will cool the atmosphere. Low-voltage halogen lighting is more true to daylight.

You can adjust the effects of natural light by providing an appropriately tinted surface for it to play on. Painting the woodwork around the window will make subtle changes to the temperature. For example, a beige paint will warm slightly and a gray will cool. When choosing, think of the colors of fire for warming tones and of snowscapes for cooling ones.

Colored voile curtains will have a far more dramatic effect on the color of the light. Throwing a small colored light up behind a roller blind, if there is room for it to be safe, or behind a screen of tightly stretched white cotton is the ultimate way of changing the temperature with light. This last method means that you may choose when you would like to benefit from the effects of natural light or a more tailored atmosphere. Another method of warming a room with light is to point a single spotlight at a gold or copper colored decorative item, such as a large plate. The reflected light will then take on the tones of the metal.

CHANGING THE ACCENT COLOR

An accent color is an incidental color that is brought in to liven up a room. It may not be the main color in the environment but is often the first color we notice. In bathrooms, the accent color is most often provided by the towels, soaps and non-painted accessories. It may also come from trimmings, such as the Art Deco room on pages 266–7. In the bright family room on pages 290–1, the accent color is the green of the replacement tiles and towels, which complements the yellow of the wall and floor tiles. Imagine this room without the green and put white in its place. It would look more stark and less energetic. Imagine that the greens were all black ...

Fashion dictates which accent colors we select for accessories and consumables. This is purely a question of current availability of things such as matching towels,

DELPHINIUM
Blue

There is a slight hint of purple in the mixture, with blue and white. A color such as this will reflect your bathwater and make it look blue and very inviting. Accessories are simple – all shades of yellow and blue are perfect partners. Try pale yellow and navy blue towels together. Or you could go for white, which will glow as it reflects the blue.

POWDER
Pink

Intensely deep powder pink is more natural than baby pink and yet still as fresh. If you accessorize with more pink, the effect will be fairly feminine and gentle. On the other hand, if you accessorize with dark grays, blues or even black, it speaks a very different language – one of daring catwalk colors and uninhibited decorators.

bath bubbles and tissue paper and does not follow a rule. It may be worth considering your choice of accent color, however, by looking around a department store before deciding. Unfortunately, where hygiene is involved so replacement is essential from time to time, we become slaves to the marketers' current trends.

CEILING COLORS

Some simple advice for choosing a ceiling color: keep it pale and you will create more of a feeling of height because the brain associates pale colors with daytime skies and openness. Darker colors are associated with the closing in of a night sky and, as such, have a lowering effect.

Adventurous, deep or intense colors can be amazing. Test a color by painting a large corner of the ceiling. Paint enough to fill your vision so that you can't see the original color. Mask the edges so that the painting comes to an immaculate, clean finish. Remember that the bathroom ceiling will be viewed for long periods of time if you are a bathing rather than a showering household.

Adding white to the color used on the walls is an easy way of making a paler shade for the ceiling. Some intense yellows, however, such as the yellow in the room on pages 290–1 may whiten up to a rather fluorescent color and it is always worth testing this first. Blues respond perfectly to the addition of a liter or so of white.

If you have a cornice in the bathroom, it can be painted the same color as the ceiling or the

walls or in a contrasting shade. Traditionally a cornice is left white but it can lend itself well to the use of a paint effect, such as marbling. It is important to remember that steam and moisture will affect a cornice – it must be treated against mold or damp before painting and should be finished with an alkyd-based paint or varnish.

PAINTING TO LAST

More than any other room in the house, it is worth spending time preparing bathroom surfaces against moisture and heat damage (see page 269). Rough or crumbling plaster must be stabilized before you begin to paint with final colors and all existing damp or mold must be obliterated with treatment sprays. Stains from previous moisture damage should be painted first with stain block. Double the amount of coats recommended on the can for use in the bathroom just to be sure.

Paint is in itself a form of sealant and plays a major role in protecting wood and plaster from steam and moisture damage. If you take care that a painted surface is painted right up to, and over, the edges, the finished effect should last as long as any other room in the house. When painting, imagine you are covering the surface in plastic kitchen wrap and that invasive moisture will get into any gaps you leave. If paint soaks into wood or plaster, add extra coats until this stops and then add a final two coats to form a colored skin.

WHERE TO WORK

Unfortunately, re-creating a bathroom takes some planning

TUSCAN
Red

Similar to the color of a sun-baked flower pot, this natural, warm tone is not really suitable for a tiny bathroom because it will make it feel even smaller. It harmonizes beautifully with cream- or champagne-colored units and, unlike other shades of red, Tuscan red is actually a soothing color.

HARVEST
Beige

When plain colors such as white and cream lose their appeal but brighter tones seem too adventurous, harvest beige may be the answer. Sometimes changing white or cream, just one step, to beige is all that is needed to bring about a transformation. Beige can be very successful against deep burgundy reds and browns.

and the usual spur of the moment impulse to change must give way to practicalities. It is a luxury to find a bathroom big enough for DIY work, such as cutting wood and setting up a work bench. Homes with only one bathroom may also be used during the day by the family. If you cannot work in the bathroom with room enough to open and close the door for privacy, set up in a room as close as possible and cover the floors of the work room and the walkway between the two with dustsheets, remembering you may need enough space to turn around with long pieces of wood. Remove anything that might be damaged and bear in mind that baths and basins may need more than one person to carry them.

Work that needs good time to dry, such as painting floors, is best carried out late at night before going to bed. This will ensure that the work is not disturbed. The only real alternative to taking the room out of service for the hours it needs to dry is to work in sections small enough to be stepped over, allowing each one to dry in turn.

Keeping a bathroom functional while major work is being carried out may be a problem. If possible, remove the basin and toilet before you begin work on a new floor and then put the replacements in after the floor is complete. The finish of the floor around the edges of the pottery will be so much better. If you cannot do this, then remember that your new pottery might be a different shape around the bottom. Tiling with thick tiles up to an existing basin or toilet will affect the height and make it

seem lower when you sit or stand in front of it.

USING HAND TOOLS AND POWER TOOLS

In most of the projects here, power tools have been used. This is purely a function of speed and a power tool is not essential. Most enthusiastic DIY'ers will gradually build a collection of power tools over time. They can reduce the time it takes to complete a project by more than half. However, power tools are more dangerous to work with and must be carefully stored with blades retracted or removed. Treat a power tool with respect and it will give years of service. If you are working late or feeling tired, revert to a hand tool. When deciding whether to invest in a power tool, consider how much you will use it and if it will pay for itself in terms of convenience and the extra leisure time it brings you. A good strong power screw-driver, with good grip, is possibly the most valuable purchase.

MEDITERRANEAN
Blue

This color will bring the sunshine to mind as it is one of the colors seen in the clear seas of warm countries. It enhances the feeling of space in any room and changes tone dramatically in different lights. Try terracotta pots against this lively color. Oranges and deep blues are also fun and the yellow of sand will add a finishing touch to the sun, sea and sand effect.

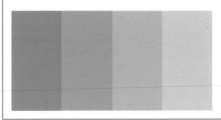

FRUITY
Green

Lime green is a zesty color that demands center stage until you light the room with candles. Only then will the refreshing push of such a bright color become mute. For a bathroom, this is ideal – fruity green is lively in the morning and relaxing if lit with candles in the evening. This shade of green cries out for red, which will stand out against it to look three-dimensional.

TILING TIPS

The tiles in this section, including the floor tiles, were all cut using the method shown on page 271 – a power tile saw was not used. However, two batches of the tiles originally selected were rejected and replaced because they would not cut well. When choosing tiles, ask for a sample to try cutting. Some are very thick and also have little 'feet' on the underside, which add to the thickness and affect the way a basic tile cutter splits the tile after scoring. The most expensive, hand-fired tiles, caused the biggest problems. The tiles used in the intricate border on pages 271 were a joy to work with and came from a basic DIY store, at a lower cost than any of the other tiles in this section.

Most of today's tiles are self-spacing, with slightly angled edges. Just butt them up against each other and the space for your grout will be made automatically. As long as you can cut the tiles easily, tiling is no longer a daunting task.

Bursting with life and zest, the vibrant blues and blocks of contrasting solid colors bring cheer to the Art Deco bathroom.

Art Deco Style

Wake up to bathroom colors as fresh and zesty as any in the entire spectrum. A blue bathroom need not take on the traditional marine or sailing themes – here is an example of where blue is brought into play with inspirations taken from the Art Deco period of decoration, though it has been somewhat simplified and brought up to date.

By way of variety, and in order to reduce potential flatness, some of the bathroom walls have been subtly colorwashed and others have

PROJECTS FROM
THIS MAKEOVER
SHOW YOU:

• *How to make a tiled*
  border
• *How to frost glass*

267

been stencilled with a simple Art Deco inspired fish design. Try to be careful not to use designs that are too brazen though because Art Deco style is able to shout for itself without too much help from you.

Most of the decorative effect of this bathroom comes from the bright tiled border around the bath, even though it was up and grouted in just three hours. This is a surprisingly quick transformation using fairly basic techniques. The result is a unique bathroom that can scarcely be ignored by guests and family.

WATERPROOFING GLAZES

The colorwash shown on the walls above the basin and toilet in this bright blue bathroom was carried out using various products that are widely available commercially. Scumble glaze is a medium that, when mixed with paint or stainers, provides a paint-like substance, which will slip and slide around on the wall surface so that it may be easily manipulated into different patterns. It is an essential ingredient for most paint effects. Of course, an alkyd-based glaze will be most suitable for use in a bathroom because it repels water – be sure to color this type of glaze with alkyd-based paints. Water-based scumble, however, has a less offensive odor and dries faster making it easier to use – you can mix this with ordinary water-based emulsion paints. Water-based glaze is already relatively waterproof once it has dried and cured but is best coated with a waterproof varnish to ensure its longevity. Apply a thin coat of varnish with a roller designed for use with gloss paints in order to achieve a perfectly smooth finish.

COLORWASHING A WALL

Colorwashing is not only one of the most straightforward paint effects to execute but also one of the most popular. The two colors used here are so very close to each other that very little effort is required on your part to create a delicately mottled effect. If you wish, you can also use more dramatic color differences but they will require a little more rubbing and perfecting so that the wall does not look as though it has been simply washed down randomly with a dye.

1 Mix the glaze using a 50:50 mix of water- or alkyd-based scumble glaze and paint – use the same base for both ingredients. These areas took a teacup (8fl oz) each of glaze and paint. The whole room would need half a liter (16fl oz) of each. If using oils, dilute with white spirit until you get a consistency of coffee cream.

2 Fold a smooth and lint-free cloth into a pad and dip it into the glaze mixture. Wipe excess glaze onto the side of the pot.

3 Now simply wipe the color across the painted walls, just as if you were washing them with soap and water. Rub any very obvious streaks once or twice more to smooth the effect. The direction of wiping will be evident in the final effect so try to keep it uniform.

Making a tiled border

MATERIALS
- paper
- pencil
- selection of tiles
- (1 box of each will fill twice the area shown here)
- tile cutter
- tile fixer
- antifungal powder grout
- rubber squeegee
- cloths for cleaning up
- duster

The most eye-catching feature of the blue Art Deco bathroom is the brightly colored border that runs around the tiles. Entirely put together with basic tiles straight from the shelves of the local DIY store, it was completed from start to finish in only three hours. The design was inspired by a complicated Art Deco border that I found in a book but it was massively simplified so that it was easy to execute and so that it still looked like tiling, rather than a detailed mosaic of smaller pieces.

Results are instantaneous; as soon as you begin to apply the tiles you will be able to see how the whole area will look and this is very satisfying for more impatient decorators.

1 Either select a design for inspiration or draw out an idea on paper. Work out the width of the border and keep it as simple as possible. Anything too intricate would be best carried out as a mosaic, see page 280.

2 To cut tiles, use a flat surface cutter and mark out the line of the cut on each tile. First, score along the line, just cutting through the tile glaze on the shiny side as shown here. Then, without moving the tile, gently squeeze the breaking arm of the cutter over the tile. It will snap straight along the line making a perfect cut. A few tiles will break wrongly but most should cut straight.

3 Cut a good supply of tiles to make your design with so that you can work speedily along the wall and see rapid results. This border used only half tiles, quarter tiles and some 2.5cm (1in) strips. Lay them out along the floor in the order that they will be placed on the wall so that you can see how many pieces of each color you still need to cut.

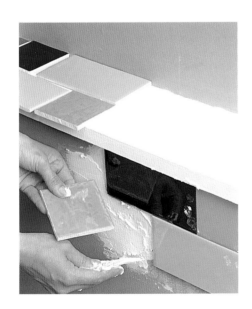

4 Apply a layer of tile fixer directly to the wall and press the cut pieces into place. Leave them to dry until the tiles do not move when you touch them.

5 Apply grout by pressing it into the joins between each tile using a rubber squeegee.

6 Immediately wipe away any excess grout and polish the tiles with a soft damp cloth. When the grout is completely dry, polish again with a soft, dry, fluffy duster.

MATERIALS
• ready made stencil
◦ re-positionable
• spray mount
• scrap paper for
  masking
• masking tape
• frosting spray

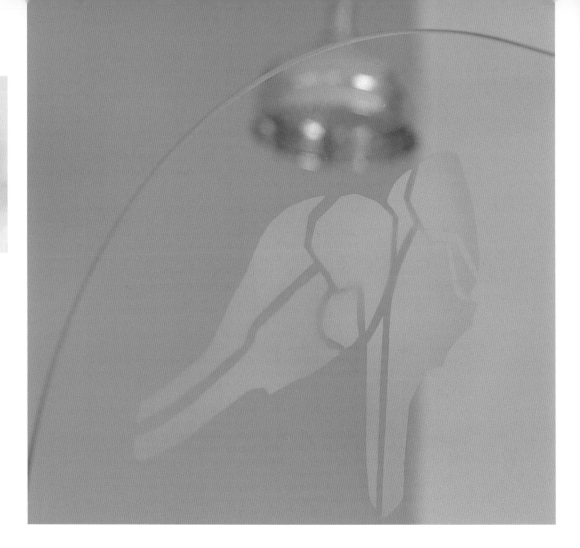

Frosting glass

Until recently, frosted glass was the domain of those who could invest good time and money in employing a professional. Now there are two methods for frosting yourself, both very effective. Supplies are so readily available from craft shops that we need no longer be daunted by the cost of gaining some decoration or privacy from previously plain glass.

One method is to use sheets of sticky backed plastic in a frosted finish and to cut pieces carefully with a knife and apply them to clean glass. The second method, shown here, is a touch more professional and definitely longer lasting. The same fish stencil that was used on the walls is used here to provide some continuity in the design of the bathroom.

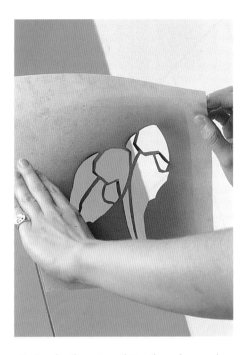

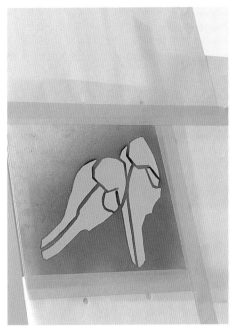

1 Apply the stencil to the glass using re-positionable spray mount. Make sure that it is fully pressed against the glass, especially if you are using an old stencil.

2 It is very important to mask the surrounding area with sheets of paper as spray travels beyond the area on which you are working.

3 Spray frosting solution lightly through the stencil and wait for a few seconds before applying a second light coat.

4 Peel back a small corner of the stencil after a couple of minutes and peek at the depth of frosting you have sprayed. You may need another coat so do not remove the stencil fully until you are sure that you have completely finished.

Soft and stylish, this is a bathroom to be proud of,
with inspiring colors and special attention to details
and the finishing touches.

Gentle lilac, blue and gray

Of all the pastel colors, lilac is unique because it

has no particular age or gender connotations and

also works comfortably as a nursery color. Here,

two shades of lilac are used in harmony with a

gentle, pale gray and white. The pure colors of the

paintwork were concentrated on in order that the

mottled tiles and the design of the floor mosaic

would be the main feature. The surfaces are

painted with satin paint and have a half sheen to

them. This includes the pale gray ceiling, which

PROJECTS FROM
THIS MAKEOVER
SHOW YOU

- *How to make swivel storage*
- *How to tile a mosaic floor*

reflects the mottling of the tiles like water.

Lilac can change color dramatically in different lights – it is a good idea to paint a large board with the shade you intend using and keep it in the bathroom for a few days before going ahead. Then you can be sure that the shade will please at all times of day.

Set into the tiles in this bathroom is a detailed dolphin mosaic, made in the traditional manner and ready to withstand as much traffic as a busy bathroom can offer. A mosaic such as this takes time and effort but will provide great pleasure and satisfaction from the moment you begin work on it.

USING GLASS

Glass is an extremely useful medium to use in the bathroom, not least because the space is often small and glass does not interfere with it. However, breakages of normal glass can be extremely dangerous in an environment where we so often walk around barefoot. As such, the use of toughened glass is highly recommended for shelving and mirrors. Not only is toughened glass less likely to break but, if it does break, it shatters into cubes and chunks without throwing dangerous shards and splinters out into the room. The process of toughening glass involves heating it to extremely high temperatures and then subjecting it to a very rapid cooling process. This makes it up to five times stronger than normal glass.

If you want to go one step further, toughened glass can always be laminated inside with a thin sheet of plastic that will hold it together in the event of it breaking. This is usual for items that are subject to high pressures and stresses, such as car windscreens but is not really necessary for the bathroom. When ordering toughened glass, make sure you order it pre-drilled with any holes you need because it is difficult to drill at home.

TILING ON EXISTING TILES

As the quality of tile adhesives is improving, manufacturers are starting to recommend that you simply tile on top of existing tiles, rather than removing old tiles to reveal an uneven surface underneath. The first thing you need to do is to replace any tiles that are missing with a cheap tile of the same thickness. Then follow these two straightforward steps.

1 Apply wall tile adhesive to the surface of clean and dry old tiles following the instructions on the tub you have bought. Make sure that the adhesive is applied evenly.

2 Working from the bottom to the top, apply the new tiles by pushing them into the wet adhesive with a twisting action. Watch out for tiles that are slipping and hold them in place. Wipe the excess adhesive off immediately as it is hard to clean up when dry.

277

Making swivel storage

EXPERT TIPS

- *If beading will not bend, try soaking it in water for a few minutes and let it dry only when it has been secured in its curved shape.*

- *Use smaller drill bits on soft pine wood than on hardboard because it does not 'give' as much to accommodate screws and requires more force when driving a screw home.*

Storage space is at a premium in many bathrooms. When you have been to the expense and effort of creating a new look, it may be irritating to have to look at some of the bathroom essentials such as cleaning fluids, cloths and mops. Here is a neat idea for storage, which tucks away into a corner and hides unsightly items when they are not in use. The corner cabinet is made from hardboard with pine trimmings. It was primed and painted using the same paints as used on the walls of the room. Casters (rotating wheels) were added after painting following the instructions on the pack. This is not covered here as the method of application varies a great deal between manufacturers. All, however, are simple to fix.

1 Cut the wood to size as follows: two 60 x 60cm (2 x 2ft) squares, for the top and bottom, which will be cut into a curved shape in step 2; one 60cm (2ft) x height required, for the upright center piece (remember the wheels will add height) and one 1.5m (5ft) x height required in flexible hardboard, for the back. Do not cut the trimmings to size at this stage.

2 To mark a curve on the top and bottom square pieces, draw an arc from corner to corner of each flat piece of wood. To do this, cut a piece of string to the same length as the side of the wood, tie a pencil to it and anchor it with your finger in the corner of the wood. Then, draw the curve, keeping the string taut. Here, the string was 60cm (2ft).

3 Cut the two pieces of wood into a curve using either a power jigsaw or a coping saw. If you are worried about not being able to cut a perfectly straight line, then cut a little further out than you need and sand back to the drawn curve.

4 Fix the pieces together only after pre-drilling and countersinking. The top and bottom (now curved) pieces are fixed centrally over the upright middle piece. Some extra off-cuts are clamped to the upright piece in order to make a wider and more stable surface to rest the unsecured top piece on.

5 Now fix the flexible piece of hardboard along the back, first with a staple gun to hold it conveniently in place as you work, and then with a few small, brass screws. The trim that will be added in step 6 will further secure this back piece. Trim off any excess using a heavy-duty knife or saw.

6 Study the completed cabinet in the photograph and add the trim along any raw edges, or anywhere you would like it. For the top and the bottom edges, use beading that bends easily. Measure and cut each piece as you work or trim after fixing. Use a drill bit that is very tight fitting and drive the tiny screws into place.

Tiling a mosaic floor

A complicated and time-consuming piece to make but worth every minute. This leaping dolphin is made up of cut pieces of traditional glass mosaic tiles. It is first made upside-down, away from its final position using a reverse method, which ensures a totally flat surface. The flat surface is very important for an area that is walked on by barefooted people. Glass mosaic is very hard-wearing and can be treated in the same way as floor tiles once it is set and fully cured (dried and set). For convenience, make the mosaic to fit the size of your floor tiles. This one was made to fit into a gap measuring five tiles wide by four tiles deep.

Gummed paper is available from any mosaic supplier. As it comes in 30cm square (1ft square), sheets you may need to join several pieces together to give a large enough area.

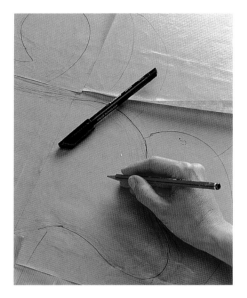

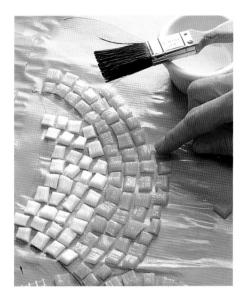

1 First, lay out a piece of gummed paper with the sticky side up. Secure it with removable spray mount or tape and draw your design onto it. Remember that your finished design will be a mirror image as it will be flipped over in step 5. Keep it simple on your first attempt.

2 Cut plenty of pieces of mosaic tesserae (squares) into quarters using a pair of nibblers – hold each piece firmly in the fingers of one hand and gently squeeze the nibblers against the other side. The piece should fracture in a fairly straight line.

3 Dampen the face-up side of the gummed paper with a paintbrush and water in small patches and then apply the pieces UPSIDE DOWN onto the surface. You can use children's water-based gum instead, but it must be water soluble because it will be washed away in step 6.

4 Next, apply a good thick layer (approximately 1cm / ⅓ in thick) of strong tile-fixing adhesive, which will also act as grouting, to the floor where the mosaic will be. Make sure the coverage is good and even.

5 Flip the mosaic over onto the floor. Moving it may cause damage so line it up before pressing the entire sheet firmly into the fixative. Use planks or a large board to press the mosaic home flat and even. Remember that it will be walked on in bare feet so must not be jagged. The fixer will fill the spaces between each piece.

6 When the fixative is dry or nearly dry, remove the gummed paper backing by soaking it off with damp cloths and polish away any excess grouting. You may need to wash and rub down the tiles to get rid of excess grout. Fine sandpaper, if used lightly so as not to scratch the tiles, will help if you need to polish further.

MAKEOVER PROJECT

Clean, crisp and pure, classic white is here paired with some tones of gray and silver for a result that is at once classic and modern.

Classic whites, grays and metallics

We all know someone who has a pure white bathroom. It gives room for decorating with changing accent colors through the towels and accessories and also reflects light and shade in such a way that makes it very practical for applying make-up easily. However, a totally white bathroom can be dull and unadventurous so here the classic white bathroom has been invigorated with the addition of equally classic grays and some metallic

PROJECTS FROM
THIS MAKEOVER
SHOW YOU:

• *How to lay floor tiles*

• *How to spray paint your
bathtub*

• *How to make a concertina
of window shutters*

283

extras. In an otherwise plain room, the eye is drawn to the effective design on the side of the bath, which softly reflects the gossamer silver of the curtain and black of the inset floor tiles. Instead of a fabric window dressing, a folding screen provides modesty and decoration and has the added benefit of being removable at times when more daylight is desired. Aside from the fact that it looks sparklingly clean, a white bathroom will be at its most vibrant during the day, taking on more relaxed yellow tones when the lights are switched on. For those who like to bask in warm candlelight, white is the perfect companion.

PREPARING TO LAY FLOOR TILES

Putting down a new floor can be surprisingly easy so long as the base on which you are going to work is sound and flat and that the tiles you will be using cut easily.

When preparing an uneven floor for tiling, the first step is to remove or grind away any major bumps in the surface. Replace uneven floorboards and re-pin any that creak and grumble underfoot. A layer of thin hardboard pinned to the floor at regular intervals is perfect to use as a base for floor tiles. Pin large sheets to the floor using a pyramid shape with the pins so that you can be sure that you have pressed it flat gradually and will not pin a bump into the side of the room. Pins should be hammered firmly into the rough side of the board so that they sink right in. Space them at intervals of approximately 10cm (4in).

PAINTING A RADIATOR

If you want to paint your radiators, you need to use specialist paints for best effect because ordinary household paints will turn yellow over time as a result of the heat. Work on a cold surface and then, when the paint is completely dry to the touch, heat up the radiator for a few hours. This cures the paint and bakes it onto the radiator's metal surface. It is amazing how much better the whole bathroom will look with a freshly painted radiator. Remember, however, not to paint the valves or the bleed screws closed as this will cause you irritation when you try to use them in the future. When you are using spray paint, be sure to ventilate the room as well as possible by opening windows and doors immediately after you have finished a coat – a breeze while you are working is likely to cause even more spray paint 'fall-out'.

1 There are specialist paints available for radiators, which are either brushed on or may be applied with a long-handled roller. A long-handled angled brush will help you to get right down the back of the radiator and into all the tight corners.

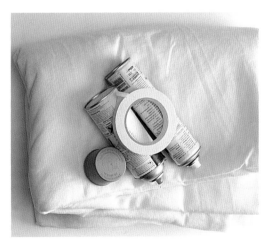

2 Spray radiator paint is very convenient to use and makes for the most professional finish. Use many thin layers, heating the radiator between each coat.

Laying floor tiles

MATERIALS
- long rule and pencil
- floor tiles
- flat surface tile cutter or tile saw
- flooring adhesive
- long straight board or baton
- tinted floor grout
- rubber grouting squeegee
- cloths

The floor of a bathroom is often neglected when re-decorating and yet the impact it has on the overall effect and comfort is enormous. A new flooring of ceramic tiles is not cheap to buy and will cost a great deal more if professionally fitted. In reality, it is more of a boring task than a difficult one, as long as you have established that your chosen tiles are easy enough to cut to size. Do this by obtaining a sample tile and testing how well it cuts.

EXPERT TIPS

- *When testing a tile for cutting ease, do it yourself. Watching a demonstration in the store will only tell you how good the demonstrator is. They may have years of practice.*

- *If you use concrete as a grout, you will need to keep the surface of the floor damp for two whole days and nights with polythene sheeting or damp newspaper sheets. The moisture is required for the curing process and without it the dried concrete will crumble.*

1 Working on a flat base of pinned hard board or cement, mark out the exact center of the room with crossing pencil lines and then lay out the floor tiles across the room in order to establish how best they will fit. If the tiles on both sides of the room need trimming, it may be wise to move the whole tiled area across so that only one side needs cutting.

2 Use good quality flooring adhesive and spread it out as far as recommended on the tub. Do not try to economize on this adhesive. Usually a liter (⅕ gallon) should be spread over 2m square (6½ ft square). Apply the tiles and press them firmly into place.

3 Flatten the area with a board or long baton making sure that all of the tiles sit at an even height and that none protrude above the rest. Work your way out of the room and leave it to dry fully for at least twelve hours. Walking on it at this stage may upset the levelling.

4 For a floor, it is best to use a tinted grout that will not show dirt as much as white. Use a mixture of sand and cement (concrete) or a ready mixed colored grout as shown here. Apply with a rubber squeegee, pressing firmly into each join.

5 Wipe the surface as you go and leave the grout to dry and cure for as long as possible – a whole day and night is best. Treat the new floor with respect for a few days while the chemicals in the glue and grout go through their curing and hardening process.

Making a concertina of window shutters

MATERIALS

- four or five panels cut to size (see step 1)
- drill and 6mm (¼ in) drill bit
- jigsaw or coping saw
- sandpaper
- paint (gray, silver and black)
- 1mm (⅟₂₅ in) drill bit
- hinges – 3 for each join
- small brass screws if not supplied with the hinges

Instead of using a more traditional method of window dressing, the clean lines of the bathroom here called upon some extremely basic carpentry skills to make a concertina of screens, which can be placed across the window when modesty calls. The height of the screens can easily be adjusted while you are putting the concertina of shutters together. These were measured against a female resident of the house and rise just to shoulder height.

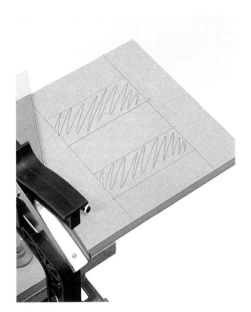

1 Have the panels (four or five) cut to size when buying the wood. We used five pieces of 1.5cm (⅔ in) thick hardboard, 60 x 20cm (24 x 8in). The total open width should be longer than the width of the windowsill so that the screens sit in a zigzag and still stretch right across.

2 Drill 6mm (¼ in) holes in the corners of the areas to be cut out and at any complicated turning points. Be sure that the holes are big enough to take the saw.

3 Now cut out each piece carefully with a jigsaw or hand coping saw. Stop at corners to turn the saw around.

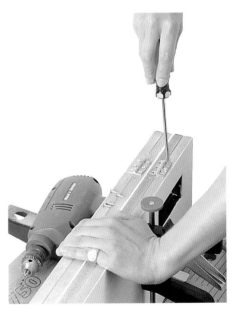

4 Sand all the edges flat and smooth and perhaps make a slight beveled edge, by rubbing away the sharp right-angled edge to a slant.

5 Paint the screens at this stage and the hinges will stay clean when you fix them. These screens are sprayed with gray and silver to go with the panel of the bath. A touch of black was added inside the cut-outs and along the edges.

6 When fixing the hinges, drill tiny pilot holes to guide the screws into position. The screws will expand to fit the holes. Test each piece and remember that you are making a zigzag so each hinge will go on the opposite side to the one before.

MAKEOVER PROJECT

A bathroom for the whole family to enjoy — fun and practicality come together for a finish that is stylish and easy-care.

Bright family colors

Decorative style sometimes calls for compromise. Nowhere is this more evident than in the home of growing children and sometimes the decor or style in lively young households can be seen to suffer. Boisterous and active lifestyles need not impede on the comfort of a home though, and a little thought can provide rooms as pleasing to adult eyes as they are practical for children.

Storage and ease of tidying will always be key

PROJECTS FROM
THIS MAKEOVER
SHOW YOU:

• *How to build a towel rail*

• *How to make a quick and*

easy toy store

aspects and this bathroom shows consideration for the adults who wish to be able to relax away from toys and clutter but also allows for children to enjoy themselves. At a glance, the shower curtain is as you would expect in any household. Inside, however, is a hidden layer of pockets and storage for bath toys. Extra shelves around the bath make the room look tidier, and provide a step for children old enough to be left alone with water. A towel or laundry rail for hanging linen on adds to the gently cluttered environment and can be pulled into the garden for drying on warm days. It is strongly constructed and will even take the weight of an adult.

DEALING WITH GROUT

Tiles seldom wear or discolor but they can begin to look tired with age because their grout not only wears but does tend to be subject to discoloring molds and mildews, which often thrive and multiply in moist and damp environments.

Grout in itself, when new, is a treatment against fungus. You can spruce grout up with specially formulated paints, which prolong its lifespan, but you will never be able to make it look as good as new unless it really is new. The best way to do this is to scrape out old grout with a knife-point, alternatively you can use a special tool that is designed for the job (grout remover), and replace it with a fresh new product. You do not have to do the whole job at once – you can carry it out in stages, by replacing grout around just a few tiles every day.

> ### EXPERT TIP
> - *When carrying out a repair such as this, the new grout may glow white against the old. It may be time to replace all of the grout for a really fresh wall.*

REPLACING A SINGLE TILE

If just a few tiles on a wall are cracked and damaged, they can be replaced using the following steps. This will make the job much easier because you will not have to replace all the tiles on the wall. In the event of a tile no longer being available as a replacement, you could also consider using several patches of a contrasting color. Make sure that you check the thickness of replacement tiles before buying them because they must be exactly the same depth in order to sit flat on the wall next to the old tiles.

1 Scrape out the grout around the tile to be replaced. This will probably be around a damaged tile but is shown here on a new one.

2 Wear goggles in order to protect your eyes. Break the tile using a large hammer with one or two swift blows. Try to crack it rather than smash it to pieces. Masking the entire tile surface will help to prevent spraying chips. Mask the edges of the remaining tiles in all cases.

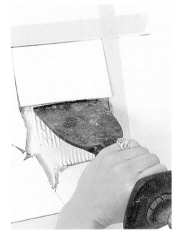

3 Remove the old, now broken tile with a hammer and chisel. Working from the center outward will help to prevent damage to the surrounding tiles. Chip away any old adhesive as far as you can.

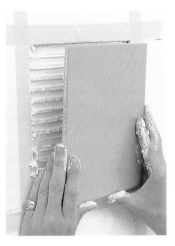

4 Add a good layer of new adhesive and press the replacement tile firmly into place. Re-grout when it is dry.

Building a freestanding towel rail

MATERIALS

- drawing paper
- pen
- set square
- jigsaw
- 2 packs of softwood lengths, 5 x 5cm (2 x 2in) and 5 x 2.5cm (2 x 1in) thick
- 2 x broom sticks
- scrap plywood
- large drill bit, same size as broom stick
- good-quality wood glue
- mallet
- few panel pins
- primer
- paint
- 4 x double direction hinges
- screws

EXPERT TIP

- *Don't forget to prime before painting. Primer helps protect the wood and also helps new paint to dry and cure fully.*

Just for fun, this free-standing towel rail is one of those things that could easily be purchased from a store but is so much more satisfying when you have made it yourself. This project is a perfect 'have a go' idea to fill a rainy afternoon; the towel rail is much stronger than it needs to be and can even take the weight of an adult. The design grew from the initial drawing and is intended to have extra pieces hinged on on future rainy afternoons.

1 First, you need to make a drawing with measurements including the height and width of each section.

2 Cut the tops and sides from lengths of wood measuring 5 x 5cm (2 x 2in) and 5 x 2.5cm (2 x 1in) thick, respectively, and cut the rails from broomsticks. Cut four fancy details for the top and bottom of each piece using thin plywood and a jigsaw for speed.

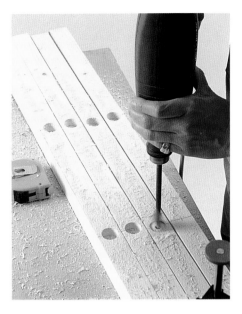

3 Drill holes for the dowel rails using a large drill bit. Do not drill all the way through the wood. Keep measuring and testing to make sure that the dowels will be level across the rail.

4 At this stage, lay all of the pieces out and test them before joining them together with good quality wood glue. Use a mallet to drive the dowels home into the holes all the way; they must be very firmly secured.

5 For extra strength, secure the end details with pins as well so that they won't give way.

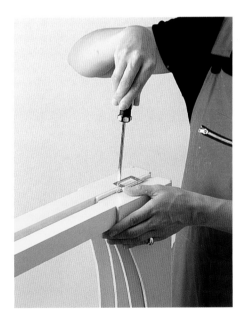

6 After priming and painting, fix hinges that open and fold in both directions by holding them in their positions against both sides of the towel rail and screwing them on. There is no need to drill a hole as the screws will make their way more firmly into the wood without holes.

Making a quick and easy toy store

MATERIALS

- 2 x identical
- shower curtains
- wax crayon
- set square
- scissors
- masking tape
- thread
- sewing machine

In a surprise toy store, neatly regimented toys wait for action behind the shower curtain. They are all in specially designed pockets from which any water from previous playtimes can drain away. Using two inexpensive shower curtains, this is a fun and easy way to provide more storage space in a busy bathroom.

1 Buy two identical ready made shower curtains to fit behind an existing more decorative one. The second curtain will be cut up to make the pockets.

2 Map out the position and shape of pockets on one of the curtains using a wax crayon in a close color (we used red to make it easy to see). Include an angled lower edge for the drainage hole.

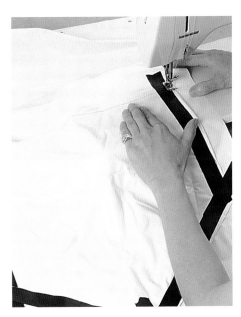

3 Place the second curtain over the first and cut it, using the lines on the first curtain as a guide but cutting a little larger than the pocket will eventually be, to allow for seams. Bring the bottom edges of each pocket down in an angle to make a drainage hole as can be seen clearly in steps 4 and 5.

4 Position the strip of cut pockets along the first shower curtain and tape it into place with the seams tucked neatly under. On fabric, this can be tack sewn but on plastic, the fewer stitches used, the stronger the final curtain will be. Sew using a machine with a long stitch, following a line next to the securing tape.

5 The bottom hole in each pocket should be tucked under about 1cm (⅓ in) and left unstitched.

INDEX

GLOSSARY

Oil-based paints	= Alkyd-based paints
Vinyl (paint)	= Acrylic latex (paint)
Matt (paint)	= Flat (paint)
Silk (paint)	= Velvet (paint)
Eggshell	= Satin
plasterboard	= drywall
mdf	= hardboard
turpentine	= mineral spirits
marine varnish	= spar varnish
architrave	= door trim
filler	= spackling compound
hessian	= burlap
China-wood oil	= tung oil
cissing	= checking

This edition published in 2004 by Bay Books©,
an imprint of Murdoch Magazines Pty Limited,
GPO Box 1203, Sydney NSW 2001, Australia.

ISBN 0-681-03142-5
Printed by Midas Printing (Asia) Ltd.
PRINTED IN CHINA.